Synonyms and Antonyms Vocabulary and Cloze

The 1000 Word 11+ Brain Boost

Part

1

The Eureka! 11+ Confidence series

CEM-style Practice Exam Papers covering:
Comprehension, Verbal Reasoning,
Non-Verbal Reasoning and Numerical Reasoning

Numerical Reasoning: Advanced Training Workbooks

Tough exam paper questions and detailed explanations of how to tackle them, to increase speed and reduce error.

Verbal Reasoning: Advanced Training Workbooks

The *1000-Word Brain Boost* is a powerful, intensive course teaching Synonyms, Antonyms, Odd-One-Out, Analogy, Vocabulary and Cloze in CEM-style questions. Its famous *Explanations* section explains hundreds of language subtleties and distinctions that many 11+ candidates find challenging.

Non-Verbal Reasoning: The *Non-Verbal Ninja* Training Course

The *Non-Verbal Ninja* is an intensive *visual* course for core CEM exam skills. The 3 training workbooks include over 600 puzzles coupled with *visual* explanations. They build both fundamental skills and the crucial confidence to seek out rules without having to have them explained first. Each book rapidly moves on from simple levels to challenging training puzzles that enhance the capacities of even the strongest 11+ hopefuls.

Please check the website **www.eureka11plus.org/updates** for updates and clarifications to this book.

Copyright © Eureka! Eleven Plus 2015. Best-selling, realistic, 11+ exam preparation series

Publication date 7 August 2015

First Published in the United Kingdom by
Eureka! Eleven Plus Exams   **www.eureka11plus.org**   Email: **office@eureka11plus.org**

Eureka! Eleven Plus Exams is grateful to Mr Dan Thomson and Ms Balbir Lehto for their assistance.

ISBN-13: 978-1515030263
ISBN-10: 1515030261

We are all human and vulnerable to error. Eureka! Eleven Plus is very grateful to any reader who notifies us on office@eureka11plus.org of an unnoticed error, so we can immediately correct it and provide a tangible reward.

Helping your child prepare for 11+ Verbal Reasoning questions

Verbal Reasoning is a cornerstone of the 11+ examination. It is intended to test familiarity with vocabulary, grammar and usage of words. The best grounding for this section of the exam is a broad and voracious interest in reading, which brings the pupil into frequent contact with a substantial spectrum of vocabulary.

In the run-up to the 11+ examination, however, the limited time is best targeted on challenging words and experience of the layout of the actual 11+ examination.

The 1000 Word Brain Boost is a series of two books, each containing over 500 CEM-style practice exam paper questions, structured into short minute training sessions, and providing answers and explanations. It delivers:

- An intense **learning workout** on words that many pupils may find difficult
- Questions laid out in modern format resembling exam papers to build familiarity
- A thorough spectrum of question types including
    - Synonyms
    - Antonyms
    - Words that do not match a specified word
    - Odd one out
    - Analogy (Similar relationships)
    - Spelling (Find the missing letters)
    - Cloze (Find the missing word)
- An answer section giving explanations including a word definition.

This intense training scheme, applied in short bursts over many days, will focus the pupil's attention on a thousand words that can prove difficult at 11+ level. To obtain the maximum benefit, please encourage your child to fill in the section at the end of each session:

- They should *list* the words they found unfamiliar.
- They should *write* a short sentence using each word.

It is important to explain to the pupil that these books form a **learning resource**, concentrating on *hard* words in the vocabulary that can come up this level. They should expect to find many unfamiliar words in each training session, and recognise this as a learning opportunity. The real 11+ exam will contain many much simpler questions: they do not appear in this intense training course.

- It is theoretically ideal to carry out the training sessions formally: pupil seated alone, away from any distractions. However, some children enjoy doing one session at a time during car journeys; seize any opportunity to exploit their enthusiasm.

- Immediately after the session, encourage the pupil to mark their own work. Immediacy and involvement increase interest – and perhaps even enjoyment – in exam preparation.

- Insist on discussing the questions which were not answered correctly. Reassure your child that the Brain Boost focuses on more difficult words, so contains fewer easy questions than the real exam. The purpose of this training system is not to predict their exam mark but to increase it.

- Most importantly, join with your child in *using* each of their own personal "unfamiliar words" in the day's conversation. Introduce discussion of otherwise-unnecessary subjects to provide an opportunity for this. This may feel incongruous, but it is better to have laughter at this stage than later bemusement in a lonely 11+ examination hall.

Once they have finished the 1000 Word Brain Boost, ask them to collate their self-written tables of difficult words from the ends of each test into a single resource. This process is valuable revision. In the final run-up to the exam you can focus on this list with them, gradually striking off words as they become familiar with them.

To see Verbal Reasoning questions in the context of other question types, we suggest the *Eureka! 11+ Confidence* series of multiple-choice exam papers:

- Question papers with the modern multiple-choice format used by CEM and others.

- Answer sheets laid out in modern format (in places requiring digit-by-digit entry)

- Full answers with explanations

- Supplementary books giving detailed methods, tips and tricks on the more challenging aspects of Numerical Reasoning

Thoughtful support from parents can be crucial for pupils in the run-up to examinations. Use the 1000 Word Brain Boost, the Eureka! Practice Exam Papers and Numerical Reasoning advanced training workbooks to help them reach their full potential.

Using the 1000-Word Brain Boost to advance your Verbal Reasoning skills

Doing the training sessions

If you can, find a place where you will be undisturbed for 10-15 minutes. Ensure the background is quiet: no TV, radio, computer, music or chat. Your adults may want to help but ask them to do this at the end of each session, not during it. Make your marks in the manner required in the exam. Below is an example.

		cАっ		cСっ	cDっ	cEっ
Example i	car	shrimp	vehicle	valley	without	hinder

Right
Right
Wrong
Wrong
Wrong
Wrong

The mark must be dark and run the full width of the box, as shown on the right.

Unsure what a word means?

Congratulations! This is an opportunity to learn. Decide which options are clearly wrong. In the real exam you should then choose the most plausible of the remaining options (since no answer guarantees no mark). During the Brain Boost, however, you do not need to guess. Just cross out the clearly wrong options as this is part of the training, and wait to read the explanation afterwards.

Learn from the explanations at the back

The Brain Boosting really begins immediately after the answering process. Read the explanations at the back. This is more important than checking whether your answer was right, because it increases your knowledge.

Brain Boost questions are deliberately tough

The Brain Boost intentionally teaches words that pupils at your stage find difficult. In the real exam and other preparation books there will be many more familiar words, but practicing words you already find easy does not boost your brain.

Build your personal library

At the end of each training session, write down the **_question_** words or **_correct option_** words you found unfamiliar or problematic.

For each word, make up your own sentence using it, as shown in the example below.

Word	A short sentence _you_ have created, using the word
surpassed	After the Brain Boost, my confidence in vocabulary surpassed even my boldest hopes.

Consolidate using your adults

Where you did not get the right answer, discuss the explanatory text with your adults. Do not be embarrassed: even adults will find some of these skill-stretching questions difficult.

Explain to your adults that you want to practice using these unfamiliar words. Build them into your conversation. This may require talking about strange things. Your adults really want you to perform at your best in the exam and will likely be happy to assist. It might even be fun!

Final revision

Nearer the exam, collate your lists of unfamiliar words from all the Brain Boost sessions. Delete the ones you have now learnt to use and produce a master list of still-unfamiliar words. Continue to work on using those words in conversation, deleting them as they become familiar.

Training Session 1

Matching Words

Identify which word is MOST SIMILAR in meaning to the word on the left. Each question has only one best answer. For each question shade your one chosen answer.

		A	B	C	D	E
1	**gravity**	mortality	attracting	seriousness	liveliness	recess
2	**derivative**	diversion	roadsign	mistake	calculation	ancestry
3	**resort**	notify	reply	spa	analysis	last
4	**ethereal**	faint	collapse	genuine	dishonest	solid
5	**espouse**	divorce	investigate	recommend	marry	cohabit
6	**extricate**	remove	yearn	complicate	mislead	formulate
7	**impeccable**	perfect	resistant	unusual	birdproof	suspended

Opposite Words

Identify which word is MOST OPPOSITE in meaning to the word on the left. Each question has only one best answer. For each question shade your one chosen answer.

		⊂A⊃	⊂B⊃	⊂C⊃	⊂D⊃	⊂E⊃
8	**deny**	repel	replicate	pony	illuminated	admit
9	**drab**	reward	musician	fascinating	indistinct	lacklustre

Words That Do Not Match

Identify which of the 5 options A-E matches LEAST WELL in meaning to the word on the left. There is only one best answer. Shade your one chosen answer.

		⊂A⊃	⊂B⊃	⊂C⊃	⊂D⊃	⊂E⊃
10	**stable**	static	barn	level	mews	desk
11	**rectify**	fix	straighten	correct	cubicle	normalise

Odd One Out

Each group has four words which can have similar meanings, and one word which is different. Find the odd one out. Shade your one chosen answer.

		⊂A⊃	⊂B⊃	⊂C⊃	⊂D⊃	⊂E⊃
12		entombing	captivating	fascinating	bewitching	charming
13		mistake	abate	decrease	subside	weaken

Go to the next page

14

cAɔ	cBɔ	cCɔ	cDɔ	cEɔ
meritorious	honourable	worthy	engrossing	righteous

15

cAɔ	cBɔ	cCɔ	cDɔ	cEɔ
exuberance	watchfulness	vigilance	attention	alertness

16

cAɔ	cBɔ	cCɔ	cDɔ	cEɔ
bear	persevere	abide	bare	endure

17

cAɔ	cBɔ	cCɔ	cDɔ	cEɔ
sturdy	sound	noisy	vigorous	healthy

Find The Missing Letters

Complete the sentence by identifying the missing letters. Write one letter into each of the large boxes below. After writing each letter, shade its corresponding element in the A-Z block beside it.

18 It was only half way through the day that I noticed the ab☐☐☐☐e of Gabrielle from the class; it turned out that she was at home with influenza.

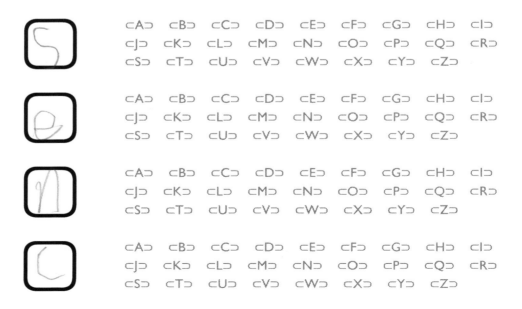

cAɔ cBɔ cCɔ cDɔ cEɔ cFɔ cGɔ cHɔ cIɔ
cJɔ cKɔ cLɔ cMɔ cNɔ cOɔ cPɔ cQɔ cRɔ
cSɔ cTɔ cUɔ cVɔ cWɔ cXɔ cYɔ cZɔ

cAɔ cBɔ cCɔ cDɔ cEɔ cFɔ cGɔ cHɔ cIɔ
cJɔ cKɔ cLɔ cMɔ cNɔ cOɔ cPɔ cQɔ cRɔ
cSɔ cTɔ cUɔ cVɔ cWɔ cXɔ cYɔ cZɔ

cAɔ cBɔ cCɔ cDɔ cEɔ cFɔ cGɔ cHɔ cIɔ
cJɔ cKɔ cLɔ cMɔ cNɔ cOɔ cPɔ cQɔ cRɔ
cSɔ cTɔ cUɔ cVɔ cWɔ cXɔ cYɔ cZɔ

cAɔ cBɔ cCɔ cDɔ cEɔ cFɔ cGɔ cHɔ cIɔ
cJɔ cKɔ cLɔ cMɔ cNɔ cOɔ cPɔ cQɔ cRɔ
cSɔ cTɔ cUɔ cVɔ cWɔ cXɔ cYɔ cZɔ

Similar relationships

Each sentence below states that one relationship is similar to another relationship. Choose the word, from options A to E, that completes the sentence best.

19

⊏A⊐	⊏B⊐	⊏C⊐	⊏D⊐	⊏E⊐
hide	hidden	revealed	concealed	display

Decrease is to maximised as obscure is to ▮▮▮▮▮.

20

⊏A⊐	⊏B⊐	⊏C⊐	⊏D⊐	⊏E⊐
minus	extra	positive	add	addition

Misnomer is to apt as subtraction is to ▮▮▮▮▮.

21

⊏A⊐	⊏B⊐	⊏C⊐	⊏D⊐	⊏E⊐
helpful	catastrophic	emergency	funeral	funereal

Death is to mournful as distress is to ▮▮▮▮▮.

Find The Missing Word

In each of the following pieces of text, one word is missing.
Complete it by choosing the one option A to E which fits best.

22

⊏A⊐	⊏B⊐	⊏C⊐	⊏D⊐	⊏E⊐
hallowed	allowed	allude	aloud	elude

It is not enough to tell me that you are reading the passage. I would like you to read it ▮▮▮▮▮ please.

23

⊏A⊐	⊏B⊐	⊏C⊐	⊏D⊐	⊏E⊐
ineffectual	effect	ineffective	affect	effete

However much the threesome strained, their skin-wrenching exertion had no detectable ▮▮▮▮▮ on the giant stone that blocked their exit.

Go to the next page

24

ᴄAᴐ	ᴄBᴐ	ᴄCᴐ	ᴄDᴐ	ᴄEᴐ
fascination	libel	foreknowledge	indecision	pencilled

When you wrote this about her, you knew very well that it was not true. In other words, this was ▇▇▇▇.

25

ᴄAᴐ	ᴄBᴐ	ᴄCᴐ	ᴄDᴐ	ᴄEᴐ
inexplicable	alternate	oscillating	alternative	uneven

The young Prince, arriving at Buckingham Palace, remarked to the journalists blocking his way, "I wish there was an ▇▇▇▇ entrance to my home."

26

ᴄAᴐ	ᴄBᴐ	ᴄCᴐ	ᴄDᴐ	ᴄEᴐ
hardback	digest	approval	annotate	consider

The plan for a new playground is wonderful news but we cannot issue this full set of plans to the public; they would find the 152 pages too exhausting. Could you prepare a 1 page ▇▇▇▇ of the key points?

27

ᴄAᴐ	ᴄBᴐ	ᴄCᴐ	ᴄDᴐ	ᴄEᴐ
never	abandon	hindsight	judgement	desist

He keeps trying to get back into the shop after being banned for stealing: we will seek a legal ruling that he must ▇▇▇▇.

28

ᴄAᴐ	ᴄBᴐ	ᴄCᴐ	ᴄDᴐ	ᴄEᴐ
items	errand	supermarket	cleaners	journey

Before I could head back home, I had one last ▇▇▇▇ to run. I was sure I could do this before the storm broke.

29

⊂A⊃	⊂B⊃	⊂C⊃	⊂D⊃	⊂E⊃
beg	attack	invite	cajole	request

She was unable to ▮▮▮▮▮ her brother Nathan into allowing her to have an extra turn on the video game that they shared.

30

⊂A⊃	⊂B⊃	⊂C⊃	⊂D⊃	⊂E⊃
torturous	erudite	tortuous	convivial	revived

I tried to show interest in their daughter's piano skills but soon regretted it when it dropped me into the trap of having to listen to one of the most ▮▮▮▮▮ recitals I have ever had to endure in my life.

This is the end of the training session.
Read the explanations at the back. In the box below, note any words you came across that were unfamiliar, together with a meaning or an example of usage. Practice using these words with adults.

Word	A short sentence *you* have created, using the word
gravity	the gravity of the situation shocked the townspeople
vigilance	the cop was vigilant of his surroundings
cajole	she was able to cajole her grandma to give her sweets.
tortuous	The sound was torturous, I had to leave the concert immediatly

Matching Words

Identify which word is MOST SIMILAR in meaning to the word on the left. Each question has only one best answer. For each question shade your one chosen answer.

		A	B	C	D	E
1	**domain**	concentrate	household	embarrassed	instruct	territory
2	**exert**	request	implicate	depart	additional	apply
3	**enduring**	instantly	meanwhile	simultaneously	finalising	lasting
4	**emphatic**	distant	definite	sliding	temperate	seductive
5	**emulate**	incinerate	destroy	delay	copy	transport
6	**extraneous**	continuous	superfluous	methodical	essential	foreign
7	**inadvertently**	secretly	horizontally	unintentionally	suddenly	hanging

Opposite Words

Identify which word is MOST OPPOSITE in meaning to the word on the left. Each question has only one best answer. For each question shade your one chosen answer.

		A	B	C	D	E
8	**domestic**	abandoned	litter	undertaken	(international)	relocation
9	**ebb**	(grow)	wane	riverbank	corn	tide

Words That Do Not Match

Identify which of the 5 options A-E matches LEAST WELL in meaning to the word on the left. There is only one best answer. Shade your one chosen answer.

		A	B	C	D	E
10	**culture**	civilisation	custom	(business)	habit	tradition
11	**dilemma**	predicament	plight	problem	difficulty	(flight)

Odd One Out

Each group has four words which can have similar meanings, and one word which is different. Find the odd one out. Shade your one chosen answer.

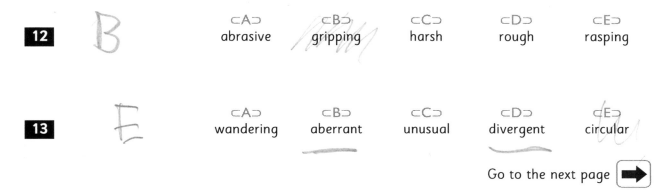

		A	B	C	D	E
12	B	abrasive	gripping	harsh	rough	rasping
13	E	wandering	aberrant	unusual	divergent	circular

Go to the next page ➡

14 _(handwritten B)_   ⊂A⊃ sheer   ⊂B⊃ extracted   ⊂C⊃ unconditional   ⊂D⊃ undiluted   ⊂E⊃ absolute

15 _(handwritten E)_   ⊂A⊃ uproarious   ⊂B⊃ noisy   ⊂C⊃ vociferous   ⊂D⊃ boisterous   ⊂E⊃ dishonest

16 _(handwritten B)_   ⊂A⊃ explosive   ⊂B⊃ airborne   ⊂C⊃ unstable   ⊂D⊃ volatile   ⊂E⊃ eruptive

17 _(handwritten A)_   ⊂A⊃ din   ⊂B⊃ harmony   ⊂C⊃ tune   ⊂D⊃ song   ⊂E⊃ melody

Find The Missing Letters

Complete the sentence by identifying the missing letters. Write one letter into each of the large boxes below. After writing each letter, shade its corresponding element in the A-Z block beside it.

18   I am not going to tell you what I was doing last weekend: it is none of your b☐☐☐ness.

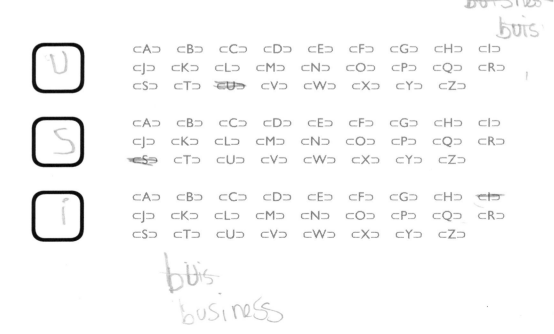

Similar relationships

Each sentence below states that one relationship is similar to another relationship. Choose the word, from options A to E, that completes the sentence best.

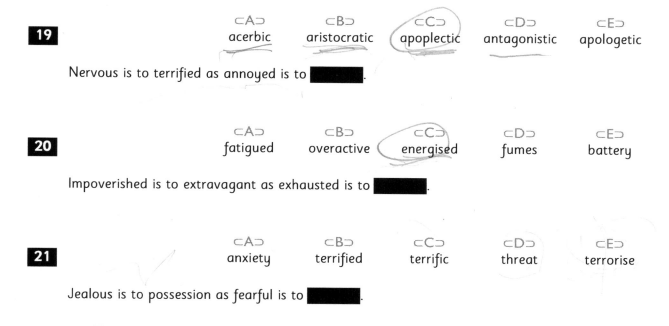

19

⊂A⊃	⊂B⊃	⊂C⊃	⊂D⊃	⊂E⊃
acerbic	aristocratic	apoplectic	antagonistic	apologetic

Nervous is to terrified as annoyed is to ▮▮▮▮.

20

⊂A⊃	⊂B⊃	⊂C⊃	⊂D⊃	⊂E⊃
fatigued	overactive	energised	fumes	battery

Impoverished is to extravagant as exhausted is to ▮▮▮▮.

21

⊂A⊃	⊂B⊃	⊂C⊃	⊂D⊃	⊂E⊃
anxiety	terrified	terrific	threat	terrorise

Jealous is to possession as fearful is to ▮▮▮▮.

Find The Missing Word

In each of the following pieces of text, one word is missing.
Complete it by choosing the one option A to E which fits best.

22

⊂A⊃	⊂B⊃	⊂C⊃	⊂D⊃	⊂E⊃
never	nibble	navel	novel	naval

The final push to maximise ship production propelled the Netherlands to the status of a major ▮▮▮▮ power, vastly out of proportion to its population.

23

⊂A⊃	⊂B⊃	⊂C⊃	⊂D⊃	⊂E⊃
manage	advise	image	remain	declare

On the basis of this blurry photo, how on earth can you ▮▮▮▮ him to be the winner of the race? It is hard to recognise even the finish line, let alone any of the runners.

Go to the next page

24

cAɔ	cBɔ	cCɔ	cDɔ	cEɔ
inherent	magnified	continual	innate	continuous

It is difficult for me to concentrate on my homework while suffering these ▮ interruptions from my younger brother. Each intrusion may only last for a few seconds, but together they stop me solving any of these puzzles.

25

cAɔ	cBɔ	cCɔ	cDɔ	cEɔ
disdain	facade	revolve	diminish	recess

Despite every setback in the first few months of running her own flower ship, Gwen's enthusiasm did not ▮▮▮. She continued with the same determination that she had shown during her years of planning, and by the end of the year, she had built a thriving business.

26

cAɔ	cBɔ	cCɔ	cDɔ	cEɔ
current	curious	currency	cursory	crossly

The security guard sorely regretted giving the helmeted cyclist only a ▮▮▮ glance as he entered the bank. Moments later, rifle in hand, the assailant had leapt up onto the bench and was barking orders.

27

cAɔ	cBɔ	cCɔ	cDɔ	cEɔ
rejoice	live	hate	recall	err

To ▮▮▮ is human; to forgive, divine.

28

cAɔ	cBɔ	cCɔ	cDɔ	cEɔ
current	currant	contain	curtain	crouton

It is not entirely true to say that we have eaten nothing: we must not forget the couple of ▮▮▮ buns we each had in the middle of the afternoon.

29

	cAɔ	cBɔ	cCɔ	cDɔ	cEɔ
	nocturnal	secretive	spurious	breaching	heroic

The ▮▮▮▮ excuses he provided, for being in the secure area out of hours, carried no weight with the guards. Soon he was bunked down in a cell, left alone to contemplate his foolishness.

30

	cAɔ	cBɔ	cCɔ	cDɔ	cEɔ
	momentary	instantaneous	conspiratorial	whisper	perceptive

After the slick sales presentation, the audience were universally delighted, except for one young man at the front who asked a ▮▮▮▮ question. The answer led to more and more questions, which eventually totally undermined the sales pitch.

This is the end of the training session.

Read the explanations at the back. In the box below, note any words you came across that were unfamiliar, together with a meaning or an example of usage. Practice using these words with adults.

Word	A short sentence *you* have created, using the word

Training Session 3

Matching Words

Identify which word is MOST SIMILAR in meaning to the word on the left. Each question has only one best answer. For each question shade your one chosen answer.

		A	B	C	D	E
1	**draft**	foolish	breeze	prepare	escape	finalise
2	**entrance**	alleyway	explain	address	hypnotise	exit
3	**discrepancy**	recitation	childhood	inconsistency	circularity	incantation
4	**ponder**	endear	reflect	mirror	drift	waterway
5	**droll**	amusing	hasten	reply	simplify	rotate
6	**debunk**	redecorate	undress	disprove	awaken	bedding
7	**proverb**	proof	highest	adverb	saying	augment

Opposite Words

Identify which word is MOST OPPOSITE in meaning to the word on the left. Each question has only one best answer. For each question shade your one chosen answer.

		cAɔ	cBɔ	cCɔ	cDɔ	cEɔ
8	**expense**	happiness	distraction	waste	income	shrinking
9	**dumb**	talkative	silence	intelligent	excoriate	deforest

Words That Do Not Match

Identify which of the 5 options A-E matches LEAST WELL in meaning to the word on the left. There is only one best answer. Shade your one chosen answer.

		cAɔ	cBɔ	cCɔ	cDɔ	cEɔ
10	**facility**	building	ease	simplicity	skill	town
11	**melancholy**	gloom	evening	sorrow	dismay	sadness

Odd One Out

Each group has four words which can have similar meanings, and one word which is different. Find the odd one out. Shade your one chosen answer.

		cAɔ	cBɔ	cCɔ	cDɔ	cEɔ
12		relinquish	abandon	renounce	discard	relegate
13		humorous	witty	fearsome	sparkling	droll

Go to the next page

14

⊂A⊃	⊂B⊃	⊂C⊃	⊂D⊃	⊂E⊃
dormant	quiescent	accurate	latent	inactive

15

⊂A⊃	⊂B⊃	⊂C⊃	⊂D⊃	⊂E⊃
credibility	honesty	integrity	veracity	affluence

16

⊂A⊃	⊂B⊃	⊂C⊃	⊂D⊃	⊂E⊃
composure	strength	vigour	force	drive

17

⊂A⊃	⊂B⊃	⊂C⊃	⊂D⊃	⊂E⊃
healthy	beneficial	wholesome	unified	nutritious

Find The Missing Letters

Complete the sentence by identifying the missing letters. Write one letter into each of the large boxes below. After writing each letter, shade its corresponding element in the A-Z block beside it.

18 Even though your name may indeed be MacDonald, your use of it on your restaurant constitutes an infringement of our trademark. We insist that you c☐☐☐e and desist from using this name.

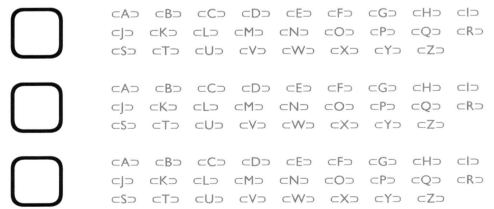

Similar relationships

Each sentence below states that one relationship is similar to another relationship. Choose the word, from options A to E, that completes the sentence best.

19

⊂A⊃	⊂B⊃	⊂C⊃	⊂D⊃	⊂E⊃
depart	liveliness	order	manure	ordeal

Enjoy is to holiday as endure is to ▇▇▇▇.

20

⊂A⊃	⊂B⊃	⊂C⊃	⊂D⊃	⊂E⊃
nonchalant	icy	burning	icicle	bicycle

Sears is to frozen as fascinates is to ▇▇▇▇.

21

⊂A⊃	⊂B⊃	⊂C⊃	⊂D⊃	⊂E⊃
promise	ancient	yesterday	yesteryear	custom

Forthcoming is to intention as bygone is to ▇▇▇▇.

Find The Missing Word

In each of the following pieces of text, one word is missing.
Complete it by choosing the one option A to E which fits best.

22

⊂A⊃	⊂B⊃	⊂C⊃	⊂D⊃	⊂E⊃
organisation	continual	registration	continuous	reduction

To qualify for the discount, Henry would have to have five years' ▇▇▇▇ membership of the club.

23

⊂A⊃	⊂B⊃	⊂C⊃	⊂D⊃	⊂E⊃
birth	both	berth	broth	brew

The ▇▇▇▇ of the internal combustion engine triggered a rapid series of innovations that within a generation left the landscape of transportation changed forever.

Go to the next page ➡

24

⊏A⊐	⊏B⊐	⊏C⊐	⊏D⊐	⊏E⊐
ocean	emulsion	illusion	omission	allusion

It seemed the sea was just at the horizon, but as the desperately dehydrated party struggled over what they thought was the last hill, they realised that this had been a terrible ████.

25

⊏A⊐	⊏B⊐	⊏C⊐	⊏D⊐	⊏E⊐
alternative	intermingle	alternate	interval	intermediate

After arguing for almost an hour over where they should hold their newly established inter-school sports contest, the opposing headmasters finally agreed to ████ between the two schools.

26

⊏A⊐	⊏B⊐	⊏C⊐	⊏D⊐	⊏E⊐
boon	victory	courage	castle	divinity

Thank you for rescuing my daughter from the dragon, good knight. As a reward, the Queen and I will grant you one ████: ask for anything you want from our kingdom.

27

⊏A⊐	⊏B⊐	⊏C⊐	⊏D⊐	⊏E⊐
bizarre	impertinent	bazaar	importunate	pertinent

As the viewers started to guess how the film would finish, the story suddenly took on a ████ twist, eliciting gasps of surprise and a few tears.

28

⊏A⊐	⊏B⊐	⊏C⊐	⊏D⊐	⊏E⊐
admirable	amenable	amble	amiable	amicable

I had heard of his reputation but in person I found him perfectly ████ and easy to get on with.

29   cAɔ   cBɔ   cCɔ   cDɔ   cEɔ
                lamented   repented   demented   cemented   depended

"When there was a proper playground here, the children loved to spend their evenings on the swings and slides, or even just chasing around the grass field. Since the council sold it, they just sit indoors with video games," ▮▮▮▮▮▮ the teacher.

30   cAɔ   cBɔ   cCɔ   cDɔ   cEɔ
                verbalise   dictation   bafflement   digression   battlement

The monologue began with a description of a trip to Lisbon but continued with one amusing ▮▮▮▮▮▮ after another until by the end everybody was in tears of laughter but nobody could remember the thread of the story.

This is the end of the training session.
Read the explanations at the back. In the box below, note any words you came across that were unfamiliar, together with a meaning or an example of usage. Practice using these words with adults.

Word	A short sentence *you* have created, using the word

Matching Words

Identify which word is MOST SIMILAR in meaning to the word on the left. Each question has only one best answer. For each question shade your one chosen answer.

		A	B	C	D	E
1	**deposit**	suggest	imagine	residue	stowaway	speculate
2	**entrance**	confuse	convergence	bemuse	inflow	doorway
3	**extravagant**	mobile	homeless	working	enlarged	elaborate
4	**coy**	lead	real	soupy	flirtatious	duplicate
5	**dutiful**	thoughtful	conscientious	regretful	attractive	overburdened
6	**desecration**	revelation	incineration	solidification	overheating	sacrilege
7	**raconteur**	storyteller	tally	calculator	ascent	competition

Opposite Words

Identify which word is MOST OPPOSITE in meaning to the word on the left. Each question has only one best answer. For each question shade your one chosen answer.

		cAc	cBc	cCc	cDc	cEc
8	**decisive**	smooth	merging	natural	sympathetic	hesitant
9	**exhibit**	dissuade	inhibit	inhabit	inside	hide

Words That Do Not Match

Identify which of the 5 options A-E matches LEAST WELL in meaning to the word on the left. There is only one best answer. Shade your one chosen answer.

		cAc	cBc	cCc	cDc	cEc
10	**extract**	essence	summary	pathway	remove	obtain
11	**complicit**	scheming	calculating	crafty	complex	conniving

Odd One Out

Each group has four words which can have similar meanings, and one word which is different. Find the odd one out. Shade your one chosen answer.

	cAc	cBc	cCc	cDc	cEc
12	implicate	design	concoct	conspire	scheme
13	extensive	persuasive	far-reaching	widespread	pervasive

Go to the next page

14

⸦A⸧	⸦B⸧	⸦C⸧	⸦D⸧	⸦E⸧
extinguished	devoured	consumed	absorbed	assimilated

15

⸦A⸧	⸦B⸧	⸦C⸧	⸦D⸧	⸦E⸧
appalling	shocking	disconsolate	abhorrent	abominable

16

⸦A⸧	⸦B⸧	⸦C⸧	⸦D⸧	⸦E⸧
undermined	dejected	wretched	forlorn	woebegone

17

⸦A⸧	⸦B⸧	⸦C⸧	⸦D⸧	⸦E⸧
clear	vindicate	support	opaque	exonerate

Find The Missing Letters

Complete the sentence by identifying the missing letters. Write one letter into each of the large boxes below. After writing each letter, shade its corresponding element in the A-Z block beside it.

18 Whatever we asked for, he said he would be able to do it. He was all things to all men: a human c☐☐☐☐leon.

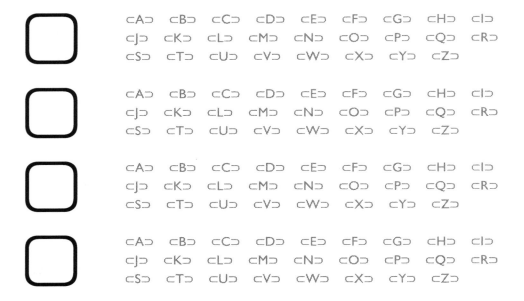

Similar relationships

Each sentence below states that one relationship is similar to another relationship. Choose the word, from options A to E, that completes the sentence best.

19

⊂A⊃ index	⊂B⊃ watch	⊂C⊃ index	⊂D⊃ pendant	⊂E⊃ wrist

Ring is to finger as bracelet is to ███████.

20

⊂A⊃ bites	⊂B⊃ scales	⊂C⊃ coils	⊂D⊃ legs	⊂E⊃ undulates

Circle is to ends as snake is to ███████.

21

⊂A⊃ freezer	⊂B⊃ embarrass	⊂C⊃ cool	⊂D⊃ boil	⊂E⊃ accept

Contrition is to deny as refrigeration is to ███████.

Find The Missing Word

In each of the following pieces of text, one word is missing.
Complete it by choosing the one option A to E which fits best.

22

⊂A⊃ credulousness	⊂B⊃ crescent	⊂C⊃ credit	⊂D⊃ crescendo	⊂E⊃ credibility

After foisting upon the villagers so many scams, Wilmer had very little ███████ left. This turned out to be a problem when his cottage really did catch fire.

23

⊂A⊃ lose	⊂B⊃ break	⊂C⊃ loose	⊂D⊃ novice	⊂E⊃ brake

In such a large group of newcomers to skiing, it was almost inevitable that someone would ███████ a bone.

Go to the next page ➡

24

	cAɔ	cBɔ	cCɔ	cDɔ	cEɔ
	misery	echo	depression	anxiety	ego

When I heard he had won this prize too, I groaned that his ▮▮▮▮▮ would now be intolerable.

25

	cAɔ	cBɔ	cCɔ	cDɔ	cEɔ
	illusion	division	delusion	elision	allusion

Demanding that all the other children play by his rules, Raymond and his ▮▮▮▮▮ of grandeur became a talking point throughout his school.

26

	cAɔ	cBɔ	cCɔ	cDɔ	cEɔ
	censor	censure	sensor	senses	cents

Hiding behind the bushes, he tried to decide which path he could take to the open window without the infrared ▮▮▮▮▮ triggering the alarm.

27

	cAɔ	cBɔ	cCɔ	cDɔ	cEɔ
	cosh	cash	crush	cache	crèche

Once the teacher had gone, I retrieved two precious marbles from our secret ▮▮▮▮▮ and we started the game.

28

	cAɔ	cBɔ	cCɔ	cDɔ	cEɔ
	ambiguous	erudite	simplistic	annoying	duplicate

"This isoceles triangle could have turned into that one by flipping upside down or by rotating 180 degrees. It is impossible to choose a single correct answer because the question is ▮▮▮▮▮."

29

	cAɔ	cBɔ	cCɔ	cDɔ	cEɔ
	implicated	condemned	torturous	contemptible	tortuous

The plot was ▮▮▮▮▮ but enjoyable because of the richness of the characterisation and depth of interaction between the hero and heroine.

30

	cAɔ	cBɔ	cCɔ	cDɔ	cEɔ
	judge	victimise	implicate	sympathise	repudiate

Joseph should be given an opportunity to ▮▮▮▮▮ your allegations, since he has waited calmly while you related them.

This is the end of the training session.
Read the explanations at the back. In the box below, note any words you came across that were unfamiliar, together with a meaning or an example of usage. Practice using these words with adults.

Word	A short sentence *you* have created, using the word

Matching Words

Identify which word is MOST SIMILAR in meaning to the word on the left. Each question has only one best answer. For each question shade your one chosen answer.

#	word	⊂A⊃	⊂B⊃	⊂C⊃	⊂D⊃	⊂E⊃
1	**capacity**	silence	reduction	loudness	whispering	volume
2	**ethic**	flowery	code	minority	scratch	idiotic
3	**erratic**	mistaken	frantic	wandering	displaced	incorrect
4	**cultivate**	mollify	intensify	clarify	discard	nurture
5	**docile**	tenth	paperwork	half-mile	medical	amenable
6	**repugnant**	vigorous	distasteful	identical	resistant	animalistic
7	**insufferable**	enjoyable	excess	painless	uninteresting	terrible

Opposite Words

Identify which word is MOST OPPOSITE in meaning to the word on the left. Each question has only one best answer. For each question shade your one chosen answer.

8	loquacious	⊂A⊃ tasteless	⊂B⊃ taciturn	⊂C⊃ arid	⊂D⊃ unexciting	⊂E⊃ solidifying
9	exterior	⊂A⊃ lengthener	⊂B⊃ fearless	⊂C⊃ shortener	⊂D⊃ abbreviation	⊂E⊃ inside

Words That Do Not Match

Identify which of the 5 options A-E matches LEAST WELL in meaning to the word on the left. There is only one best answer. Shade your one chosen answer.

10	foreign	⊂A⊃ external	⊂B⊃ alien	⊂C⊃ export	⊂D⊃ international	⊂E⊃ outside
11	incongruous	⊂A⊃ discrepant	⊂B⊃ absurd	⊂C⊃ discordant	⊂D⊃ affluent	⊂E⊃ contrary

Odd One Out

Each group has four words which can have similar meanings, and one word which is different. Find the odd one out. Shade your one chosen answer.

12		⊂A⊃ compromise	⊂B⊃ droop	⊂C⊃ wither	⊂D⊃ wrinkle	⊂E⊃ languish
13		⊂A⊃ expert	⊂B⊃ master	⊂C⊃ amateur	⊂D⊃ virtuoso	⊂E⊃ élite

Go to the next page

14

	⊂A⊃	⊂B⊃	⊂C⊃	⊂D⊃	⊂E⊃
	aggressive	vicious	virtual	virulent	venomous

15

	⊂A⊃	⊂B⊃	⊂C⊃	⊂D⊃	⊂E⊃
	dreadful	helpful	woeful	awful	unpromising

16

	⊂A⊃	⊂B⊃	⊂C⊃	⊂D⊃	⊂E⊃
	conical	usable	viable	practical	feasible

17

	⊂A⊃	⊂B⊃	⊂C⊃	⊂D⊃	⊂E⊃
	reflective	meditative	diminished	forlorn	wistful

Find The Missing Letters

Complete the sentence by identifying the missing letters. Write one letter into each of the large boxes below. After writing each letter, shade its corresponding element in the A-Z block beside it.

18 This diary will be a c☐☐☐☐icle of the events during this voyage.

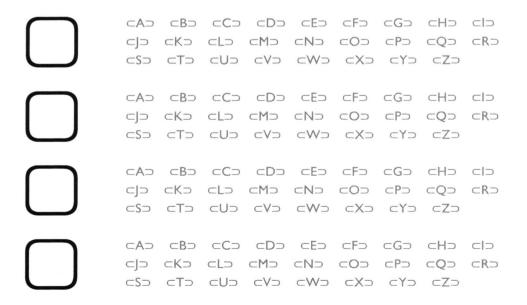

Similar relationships

Each sentence below states that one relationship is similar to another relationship. Choose the word, from options A to E, that completes the sentence best.

19
⊏A⊐	⊏B⊐	⊏C⊐	⊏D⊐	⊏E⊐
nail	bird	talon	foot	scratch

Hoof is to horse as claw is to ▓▓▓▓.

20
⊏A⊐	⊏B⊐	⊏C⊐	⊏D⊐	⊏E⊐
Britain	China	Australia	Canada	France

Eagle is to America as moose is to ▓▓▓▓.

21
⊏A⊐	⊏B⊐	⊏C⊐	⊏D⊐	⊏E⊐
freezer	break	burn	splinter	fracture

Move is to dislocate as warm is to ▓▓▓▓.

Find The Missing Word

In each of the following pieces of text, one word is missing.
Complete it by choosing the one option A to E which fits best.

22
⊏A⊐	⊏B⊐	⊏C⊐	⊏D⊐	⊏E⊐
waive	fear	terrifying	wave	dizzying

The Tower of Terror started off benignly but soon one ▓▓▓▓ of fear and nausea broke over another, until a flood of tears became inevitable.

23
⊏A⊐	⊏B⊐	⊏C⊐	⊏D⊐	⊏E⊐
except	aspect	expect	escaped	accept

I am delighted to ▓▓▓▓ this prize for the most engaging caricature.

Go to the next page ➡

24

cАɔ	cВɔ	cСɔ	cDɔ	cЕɔ
playful	intervening	mischievous	lofty	incomparable

In contrast to their ▮▮▮▮ aspirations when they set out to the trip to the historic battleground site, the children ended up, unfortunately, playing hide and seek amongst the statues and throwing stones into the nearby creek.

25

cАɔ	cВɔ	cСɔ	cDɔ	cЕɔ
angelic	equatorial	eternal	saturnine	celestial

Carefully inspecting the ▮▮▮▮ charts, the astronomer reported that the comet would pass behind Jupiter in 3 days' time.

26

cАɔ	cВɔ	cСɔ	cDɔ	cЕɔ
callous	electric	callus	clustered	calculus

Doctor Who was saddened but not surprised: ▮▮▮▮ disregard for human life was emblematic of the behaviour of the Master.

27

cАɔ	cВɔ	cСɔ	cDɔ	cЕɔ
difference	diffuse	defence	defend	defuse

With the two heads of department thumping their fists on the table and raising their voices, it required the chief executive to ▮▮▮▮ the tension by asking them to take a look at themselves in the mirror.

28

cАɔ	cВɔ	cСɔ	cDɔ	cЕɔ
descriptive	cryptic	decanted	collated	decrepit

When his answer did eventually come, it was characteristically ▮▮▮▮: I was none the wiser.

29

⊏A⊃	⊏B⊃	⊏C⊃	⊏D⊃	⊏E⊃
thoroughly	all together	vastly	terrifyingly	altogether

Leaping over the fence is one thing, but hang-gliding over the grand canyon is an ▮▮▮▮ more dramatic proposition.

30

⊏A⊃	⊏B⊃	⊏C⊃	⊏D⊃	⊏E⊃
concerning	absurdly	gatecrashing	tantamount	abusively

Your request for a refund but the right to remain in the concert anyway is ▮▮▮▮ to asking for free entry.

This is the end of the training session.

Read the explanations at the back. In the box below, note any words you came across that were unfamiliar, together with a meaning or an example of usage. Practice using these words with adults.

Word	A short sentence *you* have created, using the word

Matching Words

Identify which word is MOST SIMILAR in meaning to the word on the left. Each question has only one best answer. For each question shade your one chosen answer.

		⊂A⊃	⊂B⊃	⊂C⊃	⊂D⊃	⊂E⊃
1	**doctrine**	toilet	surgery	teaching	urinary	fruity
2	**elusive**	confusing	invisible	submerged	deceptive	slippery
3	**lucid**	enjoyable	horrific	propulsive	clear	agonising
4	**grieve**	shinguard	concise	valley	mourn	believe
5	**embroiled**	steamed	burned	trapped	laboured	discharged
6	**exquisite**	request	expel	location	perfect	disgorge
7	**slovenly**	disorderly	affectionate	beautiful	celestial	tended

Opposite Words

Identify which word is MOST OPPOSITE in meaning to the word on the left. Each question has only one best answer. For each question shade your one chosen answer.

		A	B	C	D	E
8	diluted	fluting	early	concentrated	healthy	unusual
9	duplicity	overground	uniqueness	simplicity	affluence	honesty

Words That Do Not Match

Identify which of the 5 options A-E matches LEAST WELL in meaning to the word on the left. There is only one best answer. Shade your one chosen answer.

		A	B	C	D	E
10	elaborate	intricate	convoluted	develop	overburden	complex
11	notoriety	infamy	shame	ill-repute	fascination	disrepute

Odd One Out

Each group has four words which can have similar meanings, and one word which is different. Find the odd one out. Shade your one chosen answer.

	A	B	C	D	E
12	vengeful	vindictive	indicative	resentful	implacable
13	frantic	extremist	zealot	crank	fanatic

Go to the next page

14

    cAɔ   cBɔ   cCɔ   cDɔ   cEɔ

    ewe   bull   rooster   peacock   tiger

15

    cAɔ   cBɔ   cCɔ   cDɔ   cEɔ

  dishonesty corruption delinquency corrosion depravity

16

    cAɔ   cBɔ   cCɔ   cDɔ   cEɔ

    bitter   vitriolic   acidic   delicious   vicious

17

    cAɔ   cBɔ   cCɔ   cDɔ   cEɔ

  disparage   convey   abuse   vilify   malign

Find The Missing Letters

Complete the sentence by identifying the missing letters. Write one letter into each of the large boxes below. After writing each letter, shade its corresponding element in the A-Z block beside it.

18   I promise you I paid my share of the restaurant bill. I would never try to d▢▢▢▢ve you on something like this.

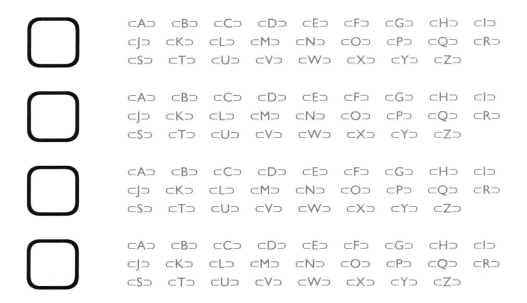

Similar relationships

Each sentence below states that one relationship is similar to another relationship. Choose the word, from options A to E, that completes the sentence best.

19

⊂A⊃	⊂B⊃	⊂C⊃	⊂D⊃	⊂E⊃
wheels	pedals	cars	cycles	road

Table is to legs as truck is to ▉▉▉▉.

20

⊂A⊃	⊂B⊃	⊂C⊃	⊂D⊃	⊂E⊃
brush	swish	guitar	tune	cleanse

Sweep is to broom as strum is to ▉▉▉▉.

21

⊂A⊃	⊂B⊃	⊂C⊃	⊂D⊃	⊂E⊃
ice	fire	dissolve	distracted	hot

Concentrated is to water as cold is to ▉▉▉▉.

Find The Missing Word

In each of the following pieces of text, one word is missing.
Complete it by choosing the one option A to E which fits best.

22

⊂A⊃	⊂B⊃	⊂C⊃	⊂D⊃	⊂E⊃
curtsy	bow	stroll	bough	branch

Geoffrey walked the full length of the ship from the stern to the ▉▉▉▉, finding nowhere that provided him with both good shade and a fair breeze.

23

⊂A⊃	⊂B⊃	⊂C⊃	⊂D⊃	⊂E⊃
implore	decide	miserable	infer	decline

Even though your offer to drive me home is very kind, I have already paid for a taxi so I must sadly ▉▉▉▉.

Go to the next page

24

⊂A⊃	⊂B⊃	⊂C⊃	⊂D⊃	⊂E⊃
disappoint	lodge	tearful	cottage	unfair

Hector's mother was extremely disappointed in the manner in which he was treated. She wanted to ▮▮▮▮▮ a formal complaint with the school.

25

⊂A⊃	⊂B⊃	⊂C⊃	⊂D⊃	⊂E⊃
cored	cord	chord	harmonium	harmonise

Having dashed through the city, raced up the staircase, and trampled their way through the auditorium, they managed to edge into their seats just in time for the opening ▮▮▮▮▮ of the symphony.

26

⊂A⊃	⊂B⊃	⊂C⊃	⊂D⊃	⊂E⊃
commit	extraordinary	unfair	burden	simple

Asking us to do questions 15 to 30 as well for homework adds an intolerable extra ▮▮▮▮▮.

27

⊂A⊃	⊂B⊃	⊂C⊃	⊂D⊃	⊂E⊃
avers	advice	adverse	averse	universe

The helicopter could not land on the ship because of ▮▮▮▮▮ weather conditions, including rolling seas and a gathering hurricane.

28

⊂A⊃	⊂B⊃	⊂C⊃	⊂D⊃	⊂E⊃
gravity	graveness	levity	pungency	descent

Six people had been killed in the "base jumping" incident. We complained to the television station that their light-hearted coverage was not appropriate: this was not a matter for ▮▮▮▮▮.

29

	cAɔ	cBɔ	cCɔ	cDɔ	cEɔ
	cyclical	collapsible	curable	collared	culpable

Having carefully examined the evidence, the judge decided that the builder was indeed ▮▮▮▮▮ for the disintegration of the tower block and enormous loss of life.

30

	cAɔ	cBɔ	cCɔ	cDɔ	cEɔ
	combative	lethargic	fascinated	endeared	controversial

Impressive though the lunch had been, it left us ▮▮▮▮▮ in the afternoon, with some scarcely able to keep their eyes open.

This is the end of the training session.
Read the explanations at the back. In the box below, note any words you came across that were unfamiliar, together with a meaning or an example of usage. Practice using these words with adults.

Word	A short sentence *you* have created, using the word

Matching Words

Identify which word is MOST SIMILAR in meaning to the word on the left. Each question has only one best answer. For each question shade your one chosen answer.

		⊂A⊃	⊂B⊃	⊂C⊃	⊂D⊃	⊂E⊃
1	**debate**	multiply	attitude	argument	reduce	interview
2	**encounter**	meet	argue	tabletop	measure	tally
3	**endorse**	finalise	equine	complete	approve	gateway
4	**horde**	accumulate	nobleman	swarm	audible	legible
5	**fallacious**	starving	embarrassing	squeezing	descending	illogical
6	**profusion**	copiousness	dispersal	synthesis	melting	confirmation
7	**loyal**	devoted	unimagined	oversized	untrustworthy	fretful

Opposite Words

Identify which word is MOST OPPOSITE in meaning to the word on the left. Each question has only one best answer. For each question shade your one chosen answer.

#	word	A	B	C	D	E
8	explicit	included	implode	implied	suck	legal
9	eulogy	refusal	correction	difference	damnation	contrast

Words That Do Not Match

Identify which of the 5 options A-E matches LEAST WELL in meaning to the word on the left. There is only one best answer. Shade your one chosen answer.

#	word	A	B	C	D	E
10	endure	withstand	persist	survive	complete	suffer
11	deprecate	discourage	condemn	disparage	denounce	demonstrate

Odd One Out

Each group has four words which can have similar meanings, and one word which is different. Find the odd one out. Shade your one chosen answer.

#	A	B	C	D	E
12	conspire	scheme	connive	plot	perspire
13	meagre	sparse	scanty	impish	limited

Go to the next page

14

cAɔ	cBɔ	cCɔ	cDɔ	cEɔ
illusory	fallacious	imaginary	specious	mislaid

15

cAɔ	cBɔ	cCɔ	cDɔ	cEɔ
zenith	apex	peak	acme	peer

16

cAɔ	cBɔ	cCɔ	cDɔ	cEɔ
peer	peak	squint	spy	peek

17

cAɔ	cBɔ	cCɔ	cDɔ	cEɔ
temperature	ardour	passion	zeal	fervour

Find The Missing Letters

Complete the sentence by identifying the missing letters. Write one letter into each of the large boxes below. After writing each letter, shade its corresponding element in the A-Z block beside it.

18 To make the coconut powder we des☐☐☐ate the raw contents of the coconut, removing all the moisture.

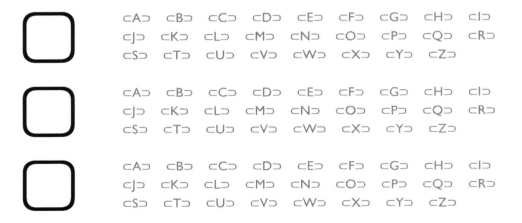

Similar relationships

Each sentence below states that one relationship is similar to another relationship. Choose the word, from options A to E, that completes the sentence best.

19

cAɔ	cBɔ	cCɔ	cDɔ	cEɔ
later	foot	pound	dollar	gallon

Metre is to inch as litre is to ███████.

20

cAɔ	cBɔ	cCɔ	cDɔ	cEɔ
bicycles	discoverer	supermarkets	machines	clever

Shop is to wares as inventor is to ██████.

21

cAɔ	cBɔ	cCɔ	cDɔ	cEɔ
network	landline	mobile	top-up	recharge

Browser is to internet as telephone is to ██████.

Find The Missing Word

In each of the following pieces of text, one word is missing.
Complete it by choosing the one option A to E which fits best.

22

cAɔ	cBɔ	cCɔ	cDɔ	cEɔ
course	curse	cross	coarse	crisis

Obtaining no relief from the conventional treatments provided in Britain, he travelled to a clinic in Switzerland to receive a ██████ of experimental injections.

23

cAɔ	cBɔ	cCɔ	cDɔ	cEɔ
broken	council	tripped	counsel	cancel

I have reported the misplaced flagstone to the local ██████ repeatedly and have little hope that it will be resolved, unfortunately.

Go to the next page ➡

24

ᴄAɔ	ᴄBɔ	ᴄCɔ	ᴄDɔ	ᴄEɔ
assent	ascent	sent	scent	assess

Without the ▮▮▮▮▮▮▮ of the head teacher, Julia would never have been able to wear the giant penguin suit instead of her uniform, during the charity day.

25

ᴄAɔ	ᴄBɔ	ᴄCɔ	ᴄDɔ	ᴄEɔ
diffident	defuse	diffuse	defies	difficult

Beyond the next bend was a small clearing in the forest, lit by a ▮▮▮▮▮▮ glow from fluorescent mosses on the half-submerged stones.

26

ᴄAɔ	ᴄBɔ	ᴄCɔ	ᴄDɔ	ᴄEɔ
address	advise	arrange	advance	advice

However much he begged for a hint regarding which route was more advisable, she remained firm in her resolve: it was entirely his choice and she would not ▮▮▮▮▮▮ him one way or another.

27

ᴄAɔ	ᴄBɔ	ᴄCɔ	ᴄDɔ	ᴄEɔ
bow	bough	boo	ballyhoo	brew

Only someone who listened carefully would have noticed that from one ▮▮▮▮▮▮ came occasional giggling sounds, as Caroline and her brother, who had clambered into the leafy heights of the tree, made fun of the appearance of passing strangers.

28

ᴄAɔ	ᴄBɔ	ᴄCɔ	ᴄDɔ	ᴄEɔ
coax	slice	imply	certify	revive

Step by step, he managed to ▮▮▮▮▮▮ the pony into the horsebox.

29

cAɔ	cBɔ	cCɔ	cDɔ	cEɔ
irritate	recognise	confuse	repeated	aggravate

Every question and request for clarification worsened the situation, serving to ▮▮▮▮▮ the new manager who was struggling to impose order on the unruly team.

30

cAɔ	cBɔ	cCɔ	cDɔ	cEɔ
brother	name	demeanour	anxious	depressed

From his ▮▮▮▮ I suspect he is going to give us very bad news about Grandma.

This is the end of the training session.
Read the explanations at the back. In the box below, note any words you came across that were unfamiliar, together with a meaning or an example of usage. Practice using these words with adults.

Word	A short sentence *you* have created, using the word

Matching Words

Identify which word is MOST SIMILAR in meaning to the word on the left. Each question has only one best answer. For each question shade your one chosen answer.

#	word	A	B	C	D	E
1	**lurid**	clear	fluorescent	ambitious	conversational	ghastly
2	**commiseration**	condolence	deficiency	complaint	description	promise
3	**depict**	eradicate	portray	admonish	leave	deselected
4	**craving**	dancing	desire	scratching	burying	embossing
5	**expunge**	mop	squeeze	rehydrate	delete	offend
6	**hallowed**	gouged	permitted	greeted	intermarried	sacred
7	**extrapolate**	project	remove	humiliate	bounce	exchange

Opposite Words

Identify which word is MOST OPPOSITE in meaning to the word on the left. Each question has only one best answer. For each question shade your one chosen answer.

		⊂A⊃	⊂B⊃	⊂C⊃	⊂D⊃	⊂E⊃
8	**ambiguous**	clear	left-handed	indecisive	underwater	skilful
9	**euphemism**	death	approximation	curse	pessimism	earliness

Words That Do Not Match

Identify which of the 5 options A-E matches LEAST WELL in meaning to the word on the left. There is only one best answer. Shade your one chosen answer.

		⊂A⊃	⊂B⊃	⊂C⊃	⊂D⊃	⊂E⊃
10	**caricature**	ridicule	lampoon	character	mock	exaggerate
11	**mercurial**	metallic	variable	inconstant	spirited	changeable

Odd One Out

Each group has four words which can have similar meanings, and one word which is different. Find the odd one out. Shade your one chosen answer.

		⊂A⊃	⊂B⊃	⊂C⊃	⊂D⊃	⊂E⊃
12		abide	bear	endure	stand	control
13		shrivel	die	perish	mutate	succumb

Go to the next page

14

⊏A⊐	⊏B⊐	⊏C⊐	⊏D⊐	⊏E⊐
retract	rescind	collect	countermand	repeal

15

⊏A⊐	⊏B⊐	⊏C⊐	⊏D⊐	⊏E⊐
amass	gather	gregarious	assemble	aggregate

16

⊏A⊐	⊏B⊐	⊏C⊐	⊏D⊐	⊏E⊐
repair	undergo	accept	receive	admit

17

⊏A⊐	⊏B⊐	⊏C⊐	⊏D⊐	⊏E⊐
weighty	serious	significant	hostile	momentous

Find The Missing Letters

Complete the sentence by identifying the missing letters. Write one letter into each of the large boxes below. After writing each letter, shade its corresponding element in the A-Z block beside it.

18 Winning the race did indeed lift his spirits. He was ebu□□□□nt as he entered the prize giving ceremony.

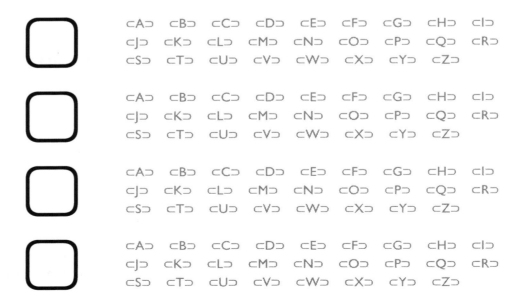

Similar relationships

Each sentence below states that one relationship is similar to another relationship. Choose the word, from options A to E, that completes the sentence best.

19

⊂A⊃	⊂B⊃	⊂C⊃	⊂D⊃	⊂E⊃
type	keys	squeak	sort	tail

Mouse is to point as keyboard is to ▮▮▮▮▮.

20

⊂A⊃	⊂B⊃	⊂C⊃	⊂D⊃	⊂E⊃
game	foot	throw	lose	actor

Card is to play as ball is to ▮▮▮▮▮.

21

⊂A⊃	⊂B⊃	⊂C⊃	⊂D⊃	⊂E⊃
corner	cube	topple	face	sharp

Vertex is to edge as edge is ▮▮▮▮▮.

Find The Missing Word

In each of the following pieces of text, one word is missing.
Complete it by choosing the one option A to E which fits best.

22

⊂A⊃	⊂B⊃	⊂C⊃	⊂D⊃	⊂E⊃
let	invite	drench	constrain	box

The danger of taking on that project is that it would ▮▮▮▮▮ you in to cover only the landscape differences between the countries; you might later find this depressingly limiting.

23

⊂A⊃	⊂B⊃	⊂C⊃	⊂D⊃	⊂E⊃
capsule	whirlpool	arbitrary	capitol	capital

An architectural, literary and scientific wonder, Paris is the majestic ▮▮▮▮▮ of the Republic of France.

Go to the next page

24

cAɔ	cBɔ	cCɔ	cDɔ	cEɔ
islet	aisle	ail	isle	supermarket

On one side stood mountains of breakfast cereal packages of all sizes and colours, and on the other was a wall of high-energy breakfast bars boasting every imaginable ingredient. It was difficult to walk down the ▮▮▮▮▮ without being tempted.

25

cAɔ	cBɔ	cCɔ	cDɔ	cEɔ
finder	astound	flounder	impress	founder

Rollo had every support we could give him but, as the pessimistic teachers had predicted, he did indeed ▮▮▮▮▮ even in everyday work, and showed no signs of excelling in any discipline.

26

cAɔ	cBɔ	cCɔ	cDɔ	cEɔ
adapt	adder	adopt	advise	adept

The zipper on her school bag broken, Susan carefully devised a way to ▮▮▮▮▮ a carrier bag for use as a supplementary cover.

27

cAɔ	cBɔ	cCɔ	cDɔ	cEɔ
bird	bridle	brood	bridal	brewed

At last they arrived at the ▮▮▮▮▮ suite, which had been specially redecorated as requested, with flowers from ceiling to floor, and studded with the finest chocolate money could buy.

28

cAɔ	cBɔ	cCɔ	cDɔ	cEɔ
parallel	bazaar	policy	bizarre	police

By half past two in the afternoon, a vast throng filled the ▮▮▮▮▮, raising a commotion that could be heard almost half a mile beyond the furthest of the market stalls.

29

	cAɔ	cBɔ	cCɔ	cDɔ	cEɔ
	effected	infected	inflicted	infested	afflicted

The new king was intelligent and just, but was ████████ by a nervous twitch of his eyes that his subjects sometimes misunderstood as surprise.

30

	cAɔ	cBɔ	cCɔ	cDɔ	cEɔ
	balmy	rummy	farm	river	barmy

"I think you are ██████," objected Isobel at the suggestion that they take turns in pulling the two ton truck up the shallow hill to the playground.

This is the end of the training session.
Read the explanations at the back. In the box below, note any words you came across that were unfamiliar, together with a meaning or an example of usage. Practice using these words with adults.

Word	A short sentence *you* have created, using the word

Matching Words

Identify which word is MOST SIMILAR in meaning to the word on the left. Each question has only one best answer. For each question shade your one chosen answer.

#	Word	A	B	C	D	E
1	sham	hoot	duck	quack	woof	roof
2	elude	finish	evade	decide	evince	convince
3	exacting	demanding	approximating	contributing	withdrawing	global
4	deride	ridicule	disembark	gallop	splinter	slice
5	exhaustive	gaseous	smoky	expelling	complete	tiring
6	gullible	dishonest	distracting	unreadable	credulous	amphibious
7	sagacious	spicy	wise	authentic	confronting	lengthy

Opposite Words

Identify which word is MOST OPPOSITE in meaning to the word on the left. Each question has only one best answer. For each question shade your one chosen answer.

8 **erroneous**

	A argumentative	B peaceful	C beautiful	D missing	E correct

9 **excel**

	A fail	B unwind	C undertake	D undermine	E understand

Words That Do Not Match

Identify which of the 5 options A-E matches LEAST WELL in meaning to the word on the left. There is only one best answer. Shade your one chosen answer.

10 **elated**

	A upstairs	B animated	C jubilant	D exultant	E enraptured

11 **sophisticated**

	A elite	B cosmopolitan	C cultivated	D amateur	E experienced

Odd One Out

Each group has four words which can have similar meanings, and one word which is different. Find the odd one out. Shade your one chosen answer.

12

	A generous	B profuse	C extravagant	D colloquial	E lavish

13

	A rebuff	B repel	C parry	D repulse	E cleanse

Go to the next page

14

⊂A⊃	⊂B⊃	⊂C⊃	⊂D⊃	⊂E⊃
deficiency	efficiency	famine	drought	scarcity

15

⊂A⊃	⊂B⊃	⊂C⊃	⊂D⊃	⊂E⊃
abdicate	relinquish	cede	liquefy	resign

16

⊂A⊃	⊂B⊃	⊂C⊃	⊂D⊃	⊂E⊃
voluntary	elective	discretionary	secretive	optional

17

⊂A⊃	⊂B⊃	⊂C⊃	⊂D⊃	⊂E⊃
annul	invalid	void	nullify	cancel

Find The Missing Letters

Complete the sentence by identifying the missing letters. Write one letter into each of the large boxes below. After writing each letter, shade its corresponding element in the A-Z block beside it.

18   My seven friends and I will divide up this cake. We will each eat one e☐☐☐☐h of it.

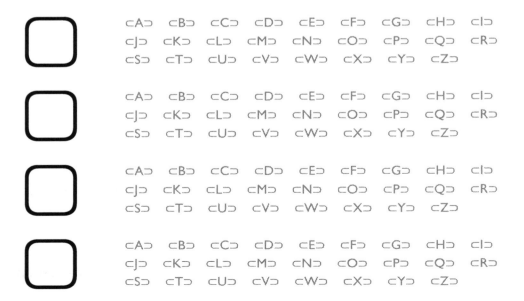

Similar relationships

Each sentence below states that one relationship is similar to another relationship. Choose the word, from options A to E, that completes the sentence best.

19

cAɔ	cBɔ	cCɔ	cDɔ	cEɔ
chance	squeeze	drop	on	handle

Press is to button as turn is to ▮▮▮▮▮.

20

cAɔ	cBɔ	cCɔ	cDɔ	cEɔ
woodwork	saw	tablet	pencil	bony

Write is to paper as chisel is to ▮▮▮▮▮.

21

cAɔ	cBɔ	cCɔ	cDɔ	cEɔ
water	fluffy	white	sky	above

Omelette is to egg as cloud is to ▮▮▮▮▮.

Find The Missing Word

In each of the following pieces of text, one word is missing.
Complete it by choosing the one option A to E which fits best.

22

cAɔ	cBɔ	cCɔ	cDɔ	cEɔ
break	role	brake	brook	roll

Somehow, in the commotion, one of the couple had dislodged the ▮▮▮▮▮ and the car was beginning to trundle forwards towards the cliff edge.

23

cAɔ	cBɔ	cCɔ	cDɔ	cEɔ
kerchief	kern	curb	cube	kerb

If he could just ▮▮▮▮▮ his hysterical approach, we might risk letting him see the boss later this week.

Go to the next page

24

	cAɔ	cBɔ	cCɔ	cDɔ	cEɔ
	written	clause	inkwell	eyesight	disastrous

I signed the contract with such eagerness that I didn't notice the fateful ▮▮▮▮ on the second page.

25

	cAɔ	cBɔ	cCɔ	cDɔ	cEɔ
	revert	despair	demise	dictate	introvert

Four more trucks passed him by, without giving any sign of recognition of his request for a lift, and Harold began to ▮▮▮▮ of escaping this empty plain that day.

26

	cAɔ	cBɔ	cCɔ	cDɔ	cEɔ
	detached	absorbed	resolved	absolved	resorted

An impressively intelligent debater, the presidential candidate was nevertheless let down by this appearance of being ▮▮▮▮ from the lives of ordinary people.

27

	cAɔ	cBɔ	cCɔ	cDɔ	cEɔ
	study	interlude	allude	elude	intercede

In your explanation please do not ▮▮▮▮ to the agreement you say you had with the previous teacher; he is no longer working here, there is no record of such any such agreement, and I do not believe extra time off will help you pass the exam.

28

	cAɔ	cBɔ	cCɔ	cDɔ	cEɔ
	asymmetry	contentment	cement	cynicism	symmetry

It is difficult to repeatedly be disappointed by the standards of behaviour and sources of motivation of others, and not let ▮▮▮▮ set in.

29

	cAɔ	cBɔ	cCɔ	cDɔ	cEɔ
	credited	credible	accredited	incredible	credulous

I am not surprised that he believed her far-fetched story. He is one of the most ▓▓▓▓ people I have ever met.

30

	cAɔ	cBɔ	cCɔ	cDɔ	cEɔ
	intention	brusque	detailed	anger	firmness

Please accept my apologies for my earlier ▓▓▓▓ manner. I was pressed for time with several people waiting for a reply to rather complication questions.

This is the end of the training session.
Read the explanations at the back. In the box below, note any words you came across that were unfamiliar, together with a meaning or an example of usage. Practice using these words with adults.

Word	A short sentence *you* have created, using the word

Matching Words

Identify which word is MOST SIMILAR in meaning to the word on the left. Each question has only one best answer. For each question shade your one chosen answer.

#	word	⊂A⊃	⊂B⊃	⊂C⊃	⊂D⊃	⊂E⊃
1	**eloquence**	series	release	articulacy	disaster	sealing
2	**deceit**	lie	recline	receipt	invoice	refuse
3	**effervescent**	luminous	sweating	fizzy	curling	devoted
4	**venal**	political	corrupt	impossible	trivial	meaty
5	**enormity**	normality	bizarreness	hatred	hugeness	disaster
6	**indifferent**	distracted	neutral	underwhelmed	matching	identical
7	**machinate**	scheme	accelerate	organisation	automate	grind

Opposite Words

Identify which word is MOST OPPOSITE in meaning to the word on the left. Each question has only one best answer. For each question shade your one chosen answer.

		⊂A⊃	⊂B⊃	⊂C⊃	⊂D⊃	⊂E⊃
8	**dearth**	birth	chilling	heavens	glut	water
9	**exhale**	inspire	reduced	solidify	accept	straighten

Words That Do Not Match

Identify which of the 5 options A-E matches LEAST WELL in meaning to the word on the left. There is only one best answer. Shade your one chosen answer.

		⊂A⊃	⊂B⊃	⊂C⊃	⊂D⊃	⊂E⊃
10	**dour**	stern	austere	gloomy	acidic	unfriendly
11	**contemptible**	intelligible	despicable	base	low	reprehensible

Odd One Out

Each group has four words which can have similar meanings, and one word which is different. Find the odd one out. Shade your one chosen answer.

		⊂A⊃	⊂B⊃	⊂C⊃	⊂D⊃	⊂E⊃
12		vivid	beautiful	countryside	graphic	picturesque
13		virtue	honour	versatile	integrity	goodness

Go to the next page

14
    ⊂A⊃   ⊂B⊃   ⊂C⊃   ⊂D⊃   ⊂E⊃
    pretty   acute   sudden   quick   instant

15
    ⊂A⊃   ⊂B⊃   ⊂C⊃   ⊂D⊃   ⊂E⊃
    harry   storm   torment   harass   distress

16
    ⊂A⊃   ⊂B⊃   ⊂C⊃   ⊂D⊃   ⊂E⊃
    subtract   material   chemical   matter   substance

17
    ⊂A⊃   ⊂B⊃   ⊂C⊃   ⊂D⊃   ⊂E⊃
    touching   abutting   juxtaposed   adjacent   adjective

Find The Missing Letters

Complete the sentence by identifying the missing letters. Write one letter into each of the large boxes below. After writing each letter, shade its corresponding element in the A-Z block beside it.

18 While the loop-the-loop was a high point of the trip to the fun-fair, it was the Flight of Fear that was most exh☐☐☐☐ating.

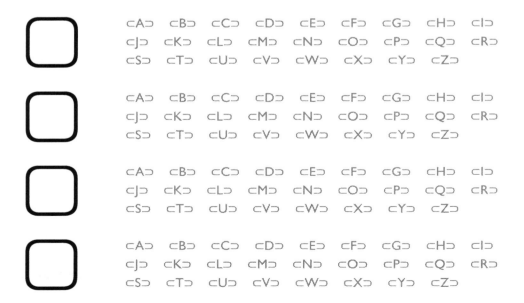

Similar relationships

Each sentence below states that one relationship is similar to another relationship. Choose the word, from options A to E, that completes the sentence best.

19

cAɔ	cBɔ	cCɔ	cDɔ	cEɔ
sphere	ball	circle	rhombus	parallelogram

Rectangle is to square as ellipse is to ▮▮▮▮▮.

20

cAɔ	cBɔ	cCɔ	cDɔ	cEɔ
horn	blast	video	music	cable

Screen is to picture as loudspeaker is to ▮▮▮▮▮.

21

cAɔ	cBɔ	cCɔ	cDɔ	cEɔ
takeoff	berthing	pilot	destroying	underwater

Airport is to landing as marina is to ▮▮▮▮▮.

Find The Missing Word

In each of the following pieces of text, one word is missing.
Complete it by choosing the one option A to E which fits best.

22

cAɔ	cBɔ	cCɔ	cDɔ	cEɔ
distraught	along	distributed	a long	distracted

Ernesto was relieved to see the finishing line was just coming into sight on the horizon. His friends and family would be arranged ▮▮▮▮▮ the final few hundred metres, and their cheers would soon would surely give him the last few ounces of motivation needed to finish the race.

23

cAɔ	cBɔ	cCɔ	cDɔ	cEɔ
popularity	comprehension	liberty	unlocked	equality

It is difficult for you outside this prison to understand the value of the ▮▮▮▮▮ you take for granted; inside here, the inmates long for it with all their hearts.

Go to the next page ➡

24

⊂A⊃	⊂B⊃	⊂C⊃	⊂D⊃	⊂E⊃
reading	indecision	cover	evening	category

I could not decide in which ▮▮▮▮ to place this book: it is part mystery, part romance and part science fiction.

25

⊂A⊃	⊂B⊃	⊂C⊃	⊂D⊃	⊂E⊃
future	founder	flounder	absentee	finder

Rollo's claim to be the ▮▮▮▮ of the institute was greeted with laughter from the many present who remember him joining it as a novice only a few years previously.

26

⊂A⊃	⊂B⊃	⊂C⊃	⊂D⊃	⊂E⊃
brooch	broom	breach	breech	broach

A beautiful ▮▮▮▮ acted as a centrepiece for the explosion of colour that was her new blouse.

27

⊂A⊃	⊂B⊃	⊂C⊃	⊂D⊃	⊂E⊃
unison	coherent	unseen	current	unanimous

Somehow we have to turn this pile of ideas into a single ▮▮▮▮ whole, so that we can win this advertising contract.

28

⊂A⊃	⊂B⊃	⊂C⊃	⊂D⊃	⊂E⊃
haddock	padlock	podcast	headlock	paddock

With one last pull on the net, they managed to haul on board their huge catch of ▮▮▮▮.

29
cAɔ	cBɔ	cCɔ	cDɔ	cEɔ
twist	irritate	aggravate	ingratiate	gratify

I carried my rucksack on my left shoulder to try not to ▉▉▉▉ the injury to my right ankle.

30
cAɔ	cBɔ	cCɔ	cDɔ	cEɔ
braggart	statue	modelling	elected	girl

I don't want to be a ▉▉▉▉, but I was voted the most handsome boy by the girls of my class.

This is the end of the training session.
Read the explanations at the back. In the box below, note any words you came across that were unfamiliar, together with a meaning or an example of usage. Practice using these words with adults.

Word	A short sentence *you* have created, using the word

Training Session | 11

Matching Words

Identify which word is MOST SIMILAR in meaning to the word on the left. Each question has only one best answer. For each question shade your one chosen answer.

		⊂A⊃	⊂B⊃	⊂C⊃	⊂D⊃	⊂E⊃
1	**entity**	boundary	completeness	being	conclusion	living
2	**enigma**	stain	brand	sketch	game	puzzle
3	**emphasis**	insistence	focus	stage	pedigree	romance
4	**venial**	corrupt	inexcusable	ghastly	impeccable	minor
5	**exclaim**	reimburse	shout	permit	allege	request
6	**indomitable**	international	bunk-bed	homeless	unbeatable	compressible
7	**debilitate**	charge	idolize	weaken	restate	contemplate

Opposite Words

Identify which word is MOST OPPOSITE in meaning to the word on the left. Each question has only one best answer. For each question shade your one chosen answer.

		⊂A⊃	⊂B⊃	⊂C⊃	⊂D⊃	⊂E⊃
8	**discredit**	promote	prepay	recapitulate	invoke	circulate
9	**hamper**	carrier	undermine	basket	assist	vegetarian

Words That Do Not Match

Identify which of the 5 options A-E matches LEAST WELL in meaning to the word on the left. There is only one best answer. Shade your one chosen answer.

		⊂A⊃	⊂B⊃	⊂C⊃	⊂D⊃	⊂E⊃
10	**eke**	economise	scream	scrimp	survive	skimp
11	**spendthrift**	wasteful	improvident	cost-efficient	profligate	extravagant

Odd One Out

Each group has four words which can have similar meanings, and one word which is different. Find the odd one out. Shade your one chosen answer.

		⊂A⊃	⊂B⊃	⊂C⊃	⊂D⊃	⊂E⊃
12		arrangement	contract	bargain	agreement	haggle
13		adverse	hostile	advertise	calamitous	catastrophic

Go to the next page

14

    cAɔ   cBɔ   cCɔ   cDɔ   cEɔ

variable   pickle   changeable   fickle   inconstant

15

    cAɔ   cBɔ   cCɔ   cDɔ   cEɔ

undercover   underhand   clandestine   clementine   secretive

16

    cAɔ   cBɔ   cCɔ   cDɔ   cEɔ

hygienic   sanitary   clean   antiseptic   sensible

17

    cAɔ   cBɔ   cCɔ   cDɔ   cEɔ

defy   flout   disregard   flaunt   scorn

Find The Missing Letters

Complete the sentence by identifying the missing letters. Write one letter into each of the large boxes below. After writing each letter, shade its corresponding element in the A-Z block beside it.

18   The death of the parakeet only days in the past, Louisa was still lost in a harrowing mist of gr☐☐☐.

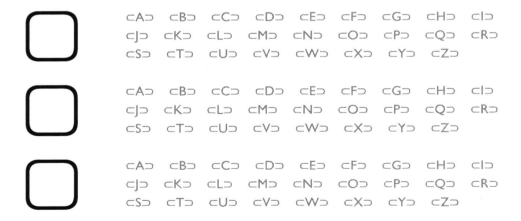

Similar relationships

Each sentence below states that one relationship is similar to another relationship. Choose the word, from options A to E, that completes the sentence best.

19

cAɔ	cBɔ	cCɔ	cDɔ	cEɔ
carrot	solidify	bake	whiskey	water

Alcohol is to tea as cake is to ▮▮▮▮▮▮.

20

cAɔ	cBɔ	cCɔ	cDɔ	cEɔ
tablet	crying	ill	laughter	prescription

Comedy is to sad as medicine is to ▮▮▮▮▮▮.

21

cAɔ	cBɔ	cCɔ	cDɔ	cEɔ
ice	water	thaw	jammed	cartridge

Printer is to scanner as freeze is to ▮▮▮▮▮▮.

Find The Missing Word

In each of the following pieces of text, one word is missing.
Complete it by choosing the one option A to E which fits best.

22

cAɔ	cBɔ	cCɔ	cDɔ	cEɔ
punish	leave	brief	delay	recognise

Come straight away to the planning room please. I will ▮▮▮▮▮▮ you when you get here.

23

cAɔ	cBɔ	cCɔ	cDɔ	cEɔ
about	advance	advice	sieve	advise

He was delighted to receive the crucial ▮▮▮▮▮▮ on choice of colour just in the nick of time, as his mouse pointer hovered over the button that would finalise the purchase.

Go to the next page ➡

24

cAっ	cBっ	cCっ	cDっ	cEっ
rotund	round	effect	around	affect

Will my rudeness to the teacher ████ my chances of being selected for the swimming team?

25

cAっ	cBっ	cCっ	cDっ	cEっ
avid	averse	avoid	avers	adverse

I do not eat prawns, nor can I even consider squid, but I am not ████ to tuna.

26

cAっ	cBっ	cCっ	cDっ	cEっ
despot	teapot	glamour	post-box	depot

The general took over and - true to form - became a ████, arbitrarily arresting and executing his opponents.

27

cAっ	cBっ	cCっ	cDっ	cEっ
include	reduce	caprice	deduce	imply

Having excluded the butcher and the baker for the reasons I have explained, we can ████ that it was the candlestick maker who was responsible for this heinous crime.

28

cAっ	cBっ	cCっ	cDっ	cEっ
engender	thrive	flourish	aggravate	evidence

Charlotte travelled around the country trying to ████ support for her plan for a charity to care for homeless spiders.

29

	cA⊃	cB⊃	cC⊃	cD⊃	cE⊃
	inspection	numerology	spontaneity	circuit	circumference

While she liked detailed advanced planning of everything, even holidays, her husband was far more interested in ███████, which was the only way he could keep interested.

30

	cA⊃	cB⊃	cC⊃	cD⊃	cE⊃
	assembly	dissemble	resemble	disassemble	similarity

Asked the reason for her visit to the country, the young woman felt obliged to ███████, concealing her unspeakable true purpose.

This is the end of the training session.
Read the explanations at the back. In the box below, note any words you came across that were unfamiliar, together with a meaning or an example of usage. Practice using these words with adults.

Word	A short sentence *you* have created, using the word

Matching Words

Identify which word is MOST SIMILAR in meaning to the word on the left. Each question has only one best answer. For each question shade your one chosen answer.

		⊂A⊃	⊂B⊃	⊂C⊃	⊂D⊃	⊂E⊃
1	**facilitate**	dedicate	assist	illegible	annoy	house
2	**equivocal**	silent	shrill	ambiguous	resounding	loud
3	**dubious**	replicated	musical	mechanical	mistaken	uncertain
4	**erudite**	adhesive	depleted	scholarly	mistaken	victorious
5	**enumerate**	count	tally	remove	catalogue	list
6	**disinclination**	reluctance	flattening	steadying	resolution	sphericity
7	**corroborate**	assist	support	abduct	rust	protect

Opposite Words

Identify which word is MOST OPPOSITE in meaning to the word on the left. Each question has only one best answer. For each question shade your one chosen answer.

		⊂A⊃	⊂B⊃	⊂C⊃	⊂D⊃	⊂E⊃
8	**degenerate**	produce	electrify	purchase	product	evolve
9	**enmity**	reception	friendship	smallness	shrinking	initiation

Words That Do Not Match

Identify which of the 5 options A-E matches LEAST WELL in meaning to the word on the left. There is only one best answer. Shade your one chosen answer.

		⊂A⊃	⊂B⊃	⊂C⊃	⊂D⊃	⊂E⊃
10	**pliant**	biddable	tractable	assenting	vegetable	compliant
11	**research**	investigate	examine	study	discover	inquire

Odd One Out

Each group has four words which can have similar meanings, and one word which is different. Find the odd one out. Shade your one chosen answer.

		⊂A⊃	⊂B⊃	⊂C⊃	⊂D⊃	⊂E⊃
12		simplistic	intelligible	easy	clear	transparent
13		flout	display	flaunt	exhibit	boast

Go to the next page

14

⊂A⊃	⊂B⊃	⊂C⊃	⊂D⊃	⊂E⊃
thrifty	careful	frugal	embarrassed	prudent

15

⊂A⊃	⊂B⊃	⊂C⊃	⊂D⊃	⊂E⊃
pompous	proud	inflated	egotistic	pom-pom

16

⊂A⊃	⊂B⊃	⊂C⊃	⊂D⊃	⊂E⊃
indict	accuse	persecute	allege	prosecute

17

⊂A⊃	⊂B⊃	⊂C⊃	⊂D⊃	⊂E⊃
torment	anguish	torture	confuse	agony

Find The Missing Letters

Complete the sentence by identifying the missing letters. Write one letter into each of the large boxes below. After writing each letter, shade its corresponding element in the A-Z block beside it.

18 Profuse apologies from Louise's friends for the noise from their all-night party did little to prevent her neighbour developing a deep g◻◻◻◻ance over the incident.

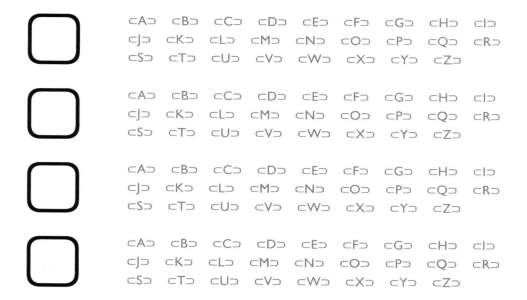

⊂A⊃ ⊂B⊃ ⊂C⊃ ⊂D⊃ ⊂E⊃ ⊂F⊃ ⊂G⊃ ⊂H⊃ ⊂I⊃
⊂J⊃ ⊂K⊃ ⊂L⊃ ⊂M⊃ ⊂N⊃ ⊂O⊃ ⊂P⊃ ⊂Q⊃ ⊂R⊃
⊂S⊃ ⊂T⊃ ⊂U⊃ ⊂V⊃ ⊂W⊃ ⊂X⊃ ⊂Y⊃ ⊂Z⊃

⊂A⊃ ⊂B⊃ ⊂C⊃ ⊂D⊃ ⊂E⊃ ⊂F⊃ ⊂G⊃ ⊂H⊃ ⊂I⊃
⊂J⊃ ⊂K⊃ ⊂L⊃ ⊂M⊃ ⊂N⊃ ⊂O⊃ ⊂P⊃ ⊂Q⊃ ⊂R⊃
⊂S⊃ ⊂T⊃ ⊂U⊃ ⊂V⊃ ⊂W⊃ ⊂X⊃ ⊂Y⊃ ⊂Z⊃

⊂A⊃ ⊂B⊃ ⊂C⊃ ⊂D⊃ ⊂E⊃ ⊂F⊃ ⊂G⊃ ⊂H⊃ ⊂I⊃
⊂J⊃ ⊂K⊃ ⊂L⊃ ⊂M⊃ ⊂N⊃ ⊂O⊃ ⊂P⊃ ⊂Q⊃ ⊂R⊃
⊂S⊃ ⊂T⊃ ⊂U⊃ ⊂V⊃ ⊂W⊃ ⊂X⊃ ⊂Y⊃ ⊂Z⊃

⊂A⊃ ⊂B⊃ ⊂C⊃ ⊂D⊃ ⊂E⊃ ⊂F⊃ ⊂G⊃ ⊂H⊃ ⊂I⊃
⊂J⊃ ⊂K⊃ ⊂L⊃ ⊂M⊃ ⊂N⊃ ⊂O⊃ ⊂P⊃ ⊂Q⊃ ⊂R⊃
⊂S⊃ ⊂T⊃ ⊂U⊃ ⊂V⊃ ⊂W⊃ ⊂X⊃ ⊂Y⊃ ⊂Z⊃

Similar relationships

Each sentence below states that one relationship is similar to another relationship. Choose the word, from options A to E, that completes the sentence best.

19

⊂A⊃	⊂B⊃	⊂C⊃	⊂D⊃	⊂E⊃
roadside	windy	downpour	airbag	forecast

Seatbelt is to collision as umbrella is to ▇▇▇▇.

20

⊂A⊃	⊂B⊃	⊂C⊃	⊂D⊃	⊂E⊃
castle	breaking	futile	dishonesty	devastation

Fortress is to destruction as promise is to ▇▇▇▇.

21

⊂A⊃	⊂B⊃	⊂C⊃	⊂D⊃	⊂E⊃
infamous	destroyed	advertise	damage	traumatising

Secret is to publicise as protected is to ▇▇▇▇.

Find The Missing Word

In each of the following pieces of text, one word is missing.
Complete it by choosing the one option A to E which fits best.

22

⊂A⊃	⊂B⊃	⊂C⊃	⊂D⊃	⊂E⊃
isle	later	alter	altar	aisle

At the front of the church, the young priest trembled slightly as he stepped up to the ▇▇▇▇ to lead his first service on his own.

23

⊂A⊃	⊂B⊃	⊂C⊃	⊂D⊃	⊂E⊃
effected	effective	affected	effect	effects

In the hope of being given a lengthy period off school, Jorgia ▇▇▇▇ a limp as she went in to the doctors office. Unfortunately for her, he had noticed her sprightly participation an impromptu game of football just minutes earlier.

Go to the next page ➡

24

	⊂A⊃	⊂B⊃	⊂C⊃	⊂D⊃	⊂E⊃
	repel	rebuttal	brutal	bridal	bridle

Jemima would ▮▮▮▮▮ at the thought the wedding would be conducted in a downmarket hotel rather than the planned castle.

25

	⊂A⊃	⊂B⊃	⊂C⊃	⊂D⊃	⊂E⊃
	increase	waive	force	wave	ways

Taking into account your extreme financial hardship, the school has decided to ▮▮▮▮▮ the usual fee for participating in the school trip.

26

	⊂A⊃	⊂B⊃	⊂C⊃	⊂D⊃	⊂E⊃
	isle	desert	ocean	shipwreck	deserted

The more we explored the tiny ▮▮▮▮▮ on which we were stranded, the more we became despondent.

27

	⊂A⊃	⊂B⊃	⊂C⊃	⊂D⊃	⊂E⊃
	due	adieu	do	ardour	ado

Without further ▮▮▮▮▮, I am delighted to call onto the stage the man whose performances have set the magic world alight - the Great Suprendo.

28

	⊂A⊃	⊂B⊃	⊂C⊃	⊂D⊃	⊂E⊃
	criterion	category	cyclist	castle	cynical

Why do you say I am not eligible for this discount? Which ▮▮▮▮▮ do you think I do not meet?

29

	cAɔ	cBɔ	cCɔ	cDɔ	cEɔ
	innocence	remorse	egotism	vigilance	comprehension

Throughout your 5 year rampage, you showed no mercy for your victims, and now standing in the dock you show not the slightest hint of ▆▆▆▆▆ for your crimes.

30

	cAɔ	cBɔ	cCɔ	cDɔ	cEɔ
	delirious	documented	delectable	doctored	declined

Don't take any notice of what I said when I was in the grip of the fever last week: I was ▆▆▆▆, suffering from hallucinations and could not think straight.

This is the end of the training session.
Read the explanations at the back. In the box below, note any words you came across that were unfamiliar, together with a meaning or an example of usage. Practice using these words with adults.

Word	A short sentence *you* have created, using the word

Training Session 13

Matching Words

Identify which word is MOST SIMILAR in meaning to the word on the left. Each question has only one best answer. For each question shade your one chosen answer.

#	word	⊂A⊃	⊂B⊃	⊂C⊃	⊂D⊃	⊂E⊃
1	**superficial**	serious	progressive	massive	international	simplistic
2	**expedient**	convenient	ingredient	curious	instantaneous	childish
3	**embellish**	exaggerate	polish	stigmatise	annotate	recognise
4	**grudging**	digging	plodding	half-hearted	sloping	striped
5	**economical**	financial	fastidious	cheap	mysterious	costly
6	**flippant**	impertinent	inversion	avaricious	talkative	revisionist
7	**exasperating**	annotating	annoying	growing	breathing	eliminating

Opposite Words

Identify which word is MOST OPPOSITE in meaning to the word on the left. Each question has only one best answer. For each question shade your one chosen answer.

		A irresponsible	B irrelevant	C untutored	D submissive	E entrance
8	**dominant**					

		A commonplace	B recent	C smoothed	D modern	E relaxed
9	**esoteric**					

Words That Do Not Match

Identify which of the 5 options A-E matches LEAST WELL in meaning to the word on the left. There is only one best answer. Shade your one chosen answer.

		A volatile	B superstitious	C changeable	D fickle	E mercurial
10	**capricious**					

		A blank	B holiday	C unfilled	D empty	E open
11	**vacant**					

Odd One Out

Each group has four words which can have similar meanings, and one word which is different. Find the odd one out. Shade your one chosen answer.

	A union	B blending	C combination	D lock	E association
12					

	A triumphant	B brave	C valiant	D heroic	E valorous
13					

Go to the next page

14

	⊂A⊃	⊂B⊃	⊂C⊃	⊂D⊃	⊂E⊃
	trickling	composed	serene	calm	undisturbed

15

	⊂A⊃	⊂B⊃	⊂C⊃	⊂D⊃	⊂E⊃
	weary	fashionable	tired	fatigued	jaded

16

	⊂A⊃	⊂B⊃	⊂C⊃	⊂D⊃	⊂E⊃
	disorder	furore	turmoil	chaos	grassland

17

	⊂A⊃	⊂B⊃	⊂C⊃	⊂D⊃	⊂E⊃
	bland	thin	unwell	insipid	weak

Find The Missing Letters

Complete the sentence by identifying the missing letters. Write one letter into each of the large boxes below. After writing each letter, shade its corresponding element in the A-Z block beside it.

18 Although he styled himself a freedom-fighter, Xavier was regarded by many as a
g☐☐☐☐illa.

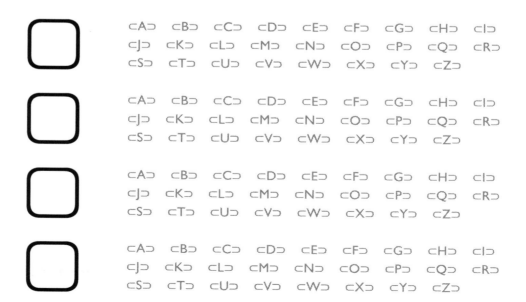

Similar relationships

Each sentence below states that one relationship is similar to another relationship. Choose the word, from options A to E, that completes the sentence best.

19

⊂A⊃	⊂B⊃	⊂C⊃	⊂D⊃	⊂E⊃
potato	metal	ladle	liquid	spoon

Chips is to fork as soup is to ▉▉▉▉▉.

20

⊂A⊃	⊂B⊃	⊂C⊃	⊂D⊃	⊂E⊃
pin	thread	threat	annoy	pine

Leaf is to oak as needle is to ▉▉▉▉▉.

21

⊂A⊃	⊂B⊃	⊂C⊃	⊂D⊃	⊂E⊃
invincible	anxious	forceful	powerful	photocopy

Duplicate is to unique as vulnerable is to ▉▉▉▉▉.

Find The Missing Word

In each of the following pieces of text, one word is missing.
Complete it by choosing the one option A to E which fits best.

22

⊂A⊃	⊂B⊃	⊂C⊃	⊂D⊃	⊂E⊃
stringent	systematic	catastrophic	civil	cultivated

However tired you are, please try to be ▉▉▉▉▉ to the staff of the hotel.

23

⊂A⊃	⊂B⊃	⊂C⊃	⊂D⊃	⊂E⊃
talkative	insular	magnetic	circular	repellent

Having surrounded the compound for over a week, the police were expecting that many of the inhabitants would give up and come out quietly, but the ▉▉▉▉▉ personality of their leader foiled those hopes.

Go to the next page ➡

24

	cAɔ	cBɔ	cCɔ	cDɔ	cEɔ
	glib	glide	gibe	glade	jibe

You say the replacement windows should cost us £125 each. This does not ▮▮▮▮ with the estimate given by your boss.

25

	cAɔ	cBɔ	cCɔ	cDɔ	cEɔ
	alludes	deludes	insides	extrudes	eludes

I had a question while you were speaking, but just now it ▮▮▮▮ me.

26

	cAɔ	cBɔ	cCɔ	cDɔ	cEɔ
	pollster	bluster	bolster	plunder	roadster

After presenting our proposal and meeting a stony silence, I did everything possible to ▮▮▮▮ our case by describing extra features.

27

	cAɔ	cBɔ	cCɔ	cDɔ	cEɔ
	financial	permit	perimeter	licence	parameter

Within the boundary of portraying the general victorious upon the mountain, the painter had considerable ▮▮▮▮ in exactly what to include.

28

	cAɔ	cBɔ	cCɔ	cDɔ	cEɔ
	crescentic	farcical	fragmentary	slimline	fanatical

The loss of exercise book, text book and all writing materials, one three separate occasions within a month, was becoming ▮▮▮▮. The teacher asked the headmaster to interview the pupil.

29

cA⊃	cB⊃	cC⊃	cD⊃	cE⊃
hostility	orchestration	ignominy	remonstration	serenity

With the conference collapsing into disarray, the princess stepped forward and, showing great
██████, led the warring factions in prayer.

30

cA⊃	cB⊃	cC⊃	cD⊃	cE⊃
electioneer	hustings	dissolution	disillusion	resolve

The loss of this election inevitably caused ███████ to set in among the campaign group;
nevertheless Toberick showed his leadership skills yet again by spinning a tale of future success
that brought back into harness to prepare for the next one.

This is the end of the training session.
Read the explanations at the back. In the box below, note any words you came across that
were unfamiliar, together with a meaning or an example of usage. Practice using these words
with adults.

Word	A short sentence *you* have created, using the word

Matching Words

Identify which word is MOST SIMILAR in meaning to the word on the left. Each question has only one best answer. For each question shade your one chosen answer.

#	word	cAɔ	cBɔ	cCɔ	cDɔ	cEɔ
1	exploit	destroy	exaggeration	exploration	detonate	utilise
2	decadent	elegant	reluctant	ancient	degenerate	prolonged
3	magnate	attractor	metalloid	network	tycoon	adhesive
4	crass	sophisticated	insensitive	copious	verdant	green
5	exuberance	roadways	majestic	collection	hypnosis	effervescence
6	insurmountable	inaudible	exaggerated	low-altitude	unpredictable	overwhelming
7	equivocate	decide	sing	prevaricate	scream	distinguish

Opposite Words

Identify which word is MOST OPPOSITE in meaning to the word on the left. Each question has only one best answer. For each question shade your one chosen answer.

		⊂A⊃	⊂B⊃	⊂C⊃	⊂D⊃	⊂E⊃
8	**exemplary**	awful	entrance	minimised	religious	decelerating
9	**denounce**	catalogue	represent	cancel	glorify	conceal

Words That Do Not Match

Identify which of the 5 options A-E matches LEAST WELL in meaning to the word on the left. There is only one best answer. Shade your one chosen answer.

		⊂A⊃	⊂B⊃	⊂C⊃	⊂D⊃	⊂E⊃
10	**endeavour**	effort	activity	attempt	finish	try
11	**sycophant**	mentalist	fawner	groveller	flatterer	toady

Odd One Out

Each group has four words which can have similar meanings, and one word which is different. Find the odd one out. Shade your one chosen answer.

	⊂A⊃	⊂B⊃	⊂C⊃	⊂D⊃	⊂E⊃
12	stubborn	inflexible	oblique	obstinate	unbending
13	language	dialect	tongue	mouth	speech

Go to the next page

14
⊂A⊃	⊂B⊃	⊂C⊃	⊂D⊃	⊂E⊃
timid	retiring	violent	bashful	restrained

15
⊂A⊃	⊂B⊃	⊂C⊃	⊂D⊃	⊂E⊃
anxiety	understanding	unease	apprehension	misgiving

16
⊂A⊃	⊂B⊃	⊂C⊃	⊂D⊃	⊂E⊃
impenetrable	subtle	imperceptible	hidden	microscopic

17
⊂A⊃	⊂B⊃	⊂C⊃	⊂D⊃	⊂E⊃
average	unimportant	indifferent	mediocre	identical

Find The Missing Letters

Complete the sentence by identifying the missing letters. Write one letter into each of the large boxes below. After writing each letter, shade its corresponding element in the A-Z block beside it.

18 Their discovery that they had accidentally left the picnic hamper at home did not daunt the foursome. After all, they did manage to bring two bananas; they could simply h☐☐☐e each one and thus each have an equal share.

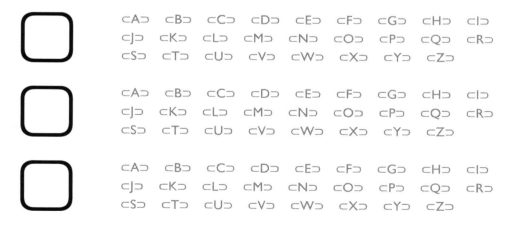

Similar relationships

Each sentence below states that one relationship is similar to another relationship. Choose the word, from options A to E, that completes the sentence best.

19

⊂A⊃	⊂B⊃	⊂C⊃	⊂D⊃	⊂E⊃
parcel	orange	letter	squeeze	bottle

Carton is to juice as envelope is to ▮▮▮▮▮▮.

20

⊂A⊃	⊂B⊃	⊂C⊃	⊂D⊃	⊂E⊃
apple	hamburger	computer	rain	pear

Shade is to sunlight as mackintosh is to ▮▮▮▮▮▮.

21

⊂A⊃	⊂B⊃	⊂C⊃	⊂D⊃	⊂E⊃
baffle	waffle	ingest	enquire	satisfied

Puzzled is to investigate as starved is to ▮▮▮▮▮▮.

Find The Missing Word

In each of the following pieces of text, one word is missing.
Complete it by choosing the one option A to E which fits best.

22

⊂A⊃	⊂B⊃	⊂C⊃	⊂D⊃	⊂E⊃
inviting	incremental	liberal	collegial	precise

Although we started with a very strict set of criteria for joining this club, over the years we have become far more ▮▮▮▮▮▮.

23

⊂A⊃	⊂B⊃	⊂C⊃	⊂D⊃	⊂E⊃
curtain	stream	currant	flooding	current

Although it looks tempting to take a dip in this river, beware the ▮▮▮▮▮▮, which is far stronger than you might assume.

Go to the next page

24

cAc	cBc	cCc	cDc	cEc
frieze	ascendant	freeze	fleece	above

Upstairs you will see the glorious and intricate Andromeda ▮▮▮▮, depicting the discovery of fire by early humans.

25

cAc	cBc	cCc	cDc	cEc
dessert	serve	desert	deserve	deserted

We partook so greedily in the main meal that when the ▮▮▮▮ selection arrived, scarcely anyone could face a single morsel more.

26

cAc	cBc	cCc	cDc	cEc
cryptic	vegetable	cynic	vegetarian	Cyrillic

After years of observing the behaviour of people selling their latest miracle cure, I have become a ▮▮▮▮.

27

cAc	cBc	cCc	cDc	cEc
arrest	understand	imprison	listen	delineate

I must ask you to ▮▮▮▮ your exact reasons for believing your son is in our police cell.

28

cAc	cBc	cCc	cDc	cEc
collapsed	stagnant	invisible	reversed	exploded

After twenty years of rapid growth, the town was hit by the worldwide recession and its economy became ▮▮▮▮, with few new businesses being opened from season to season, and none of the traffic jams which were commonplace in its rising years.

29

	⊂A⊃	⊂B⊃	⊂C⊃	⊂D⊃	⊂E⊃
	underhand	disappear	audible	appear	chortle

"I heard someone ███████ when I went through my new proposal for the school song; everyone is going to stay here until they identify themselves," announced the headmaster crossly.

30

	⊂A⊃	⊂B⊃	⊂C⊃	⊂D⊃	⊂E⊃
	instance	typical	condone	exemplify	impair

In your film on road safety, please could you show some cases of accidents that occurred and were just prevented? The case stories should ██████ both good and bad practice.

_____

This is the end of the training session.
Read the explanations at the back. In the box below, note any words you came across that were unfamiliar, together with a meaning or an example of usage. Practice using these words with adults.

Word	A short sentence *you* have created, using the word

Matching Words

Identify which word is MOST SIMILAR in meaning to the word on the left. Each question has only one best answer. For each question shade your one chosen answer.

		A	B	C	D	E
1	**ethnic**	spicy	colourful	distant	tribal	global
2	**denote**	erase	forget	annotate	unstick	mean
3	**esteem**	permission	overflow	overheat	regard	combine
4	**enchanting**	assisting	repellent	gasping	beautiful	harmonious
5	**egotistical**	mathematical	selfish	atmospheric	digital	unlikely
6	**nauseating**	standing	collapsing	levelling	furniture	revolting
7	**dishevelled**	untidy	homeless	uneven	overgrown	discarded

Opposite Words

Identify which word is MOST OPPOSITE in meaning to the word on the left. Each question has only one best answer. For each question shade your one chosen answer.

		⊂A⊃	⊂B⊃	⊂C⊃	⊂D⊃	⊂E⊃
8	**ambivalent**	drownable	decisive	dextrous	destitute	unconfident
9	**decorum**	untidiness	disarray	rudeness	inaccuracy	existence

Words That Do Not Match

Identify which of the 5 options A-E matches LEAST WELL in meaning to the word on the left. There is only one best answer. Shade your one chosen answer.

		⊂A⊃	⊂B⊃	⊂C⊃	⊂D⊃	⊂E⊃
10	**reflective**	contagious	thoughtful	pensive	contemplative	introspective
11	**rapacious**	salacious	ravenous	grasping	voracious	greedy

Odd One Out

Each group has four words which can have similar meanings, and one word which is different. Find the odd one out. Shade your one chosen answer.

	⊂A⊃	⊂B⊃	⊂C⊃	⊂D⊃	⊂E⊃
12	decade	flimsy	tenuous	slender	insubstantial
13	disturbing	bothersome	troublesome	pester	annoying

Go to the next page

14

⊂A⊃	⊂B⊃	⊂C⊃	⊂D⊃	⊂E⊃
illegal	formidable	threatening	menacing	fearful

15

⊂A⊃	⊂B⊃	⊂C⊃	⊂D⊃	⊂E⊃
mild	atlantic	pacific	meek	gentle

16

⊂A⊃	⊂B⊃	⊂C⊃	⊂D⊃	⊂E⊃
ultimate	unbeatable	extreme	ultimatum	supreme

17

⊂A⊃	⊂B⊃	⊂C⊃	⊂D⊃	⊂E⊃
misplace	remove	displace	transport	reposition

Find The Missing Letters

Complete the sentence by identifying the missing letters. Write one letter into each of the large boxes below. After writing each letter, shade its corresponding element in the A-Z block beside it.

18 Seeing Jeremy leaning forward from his driving position behind the low carriage, resplendent in his fine new costume, Michelle could not help but notice how ha☐☐☐☐me he was.

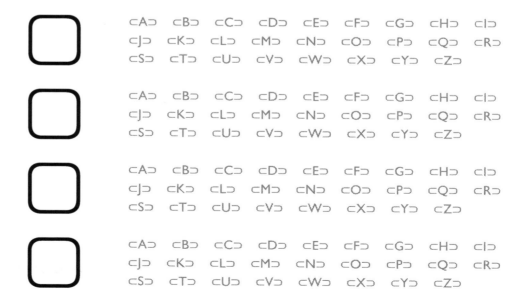

Similar relationships

Each sentence below states that one relationship is similar to another relationship. Choose the word, from options A to E, that completes the sentence best.

19

cAɔ	cBɔ	cCɔ	cDɔ	cEɔ
water	danger	electrocute	leak	waste

Spark is to electricity as drip is to ▇▇▇.

20

cAɔ	cBɔ	cCɔ	cDɔ	cEɔ
stories	memorise	play	storey	memories

Book is to page as skyscraper is to ▇▇▇.

21

cAɔ	cBɔ	cCɔ	cDɔ	cEɔ
silent	shirking	exploded	implode	rectify

Rotating is to stationary as booming is to ▇▇▇.

Find The Missing Word

In each of the following pieces of text, one word is missing.
Complete it by choosing the one option A to E which fits best.

22

cAɔ	cBɔ	cCɔ	cDɔ	cEɔ
alter	discard	altar	halter	replace

Six months of fine dining had not been kind to Akiko's waistline. She decided it was time to ▇▇▇ her dresses so she could still fit into them.

23

cAɔ	cBɔ	cCɔ	cDɔ	cEɔ
canine	another	assistant	caution	helper

"Danger: Scaffolding above. Enter area with ▇▇▇."

Go to the next page ➡

24

cAɔ	cBɔ	cCɔ	cDɔ	cEɔ
threes	freeze	trees	frees	frieze

How am I supposed to survive out here in the snow and ice? I will surely ▮▮▮▮▮.

25

cAɔ	cBɔ	cCɔ	cDɔ	cEɔ
innocent	terrified	aberrant	quivering	abhorrent

Step by step, her mother helped Agnes correct her ▮▮▮▮▮ pronunciation of the difficult dinosaur names.

26

cAɔ	cBɔ	cCɔ	cDɔ	cEɔ
grisly	gristly	darkly	darkened	grizzly

When she turned the light on, the scene of the murder was so ▮▮▮▮▮ that Sarah recoiled, overcome with a sense of nausea.

27

cAɔ	cBɔ	cCɔ	cDɔ	cEɔ
debating	ignoring	publicising	brooding	devising

Ever since the public dispute last year, she has been quietly ▮▮▮▮▮ a hatred of him.

28

cAɔ	cBɔ	cCɔ	cDɔ	cEɔ
instant	snoozing	climatic	exaggerated	climactic

The ▮▮▮▮▮ moment of the game was a long shot where the ball teetered on the edge of the basketball ring and, with the crowd gasping, tipped forward, registering the winning point.

29

cAɔ	cBɔ	cCɔ	cDɔ	cEɔ
idolatry	rigorousness	independence	freedom	poignancy

Seeing the flag being finally draped over the coffin of the young soldier, I was moved by the ▮▮▮▮▮ of that image, which stayed in my mind for years.

30

cAɔ	cBɔ	cCɔ	cDɔ	cEɔ
routine	saddening	enthralling	uninspiring	rambling

His experiences of getting into, and out of, major difficulties while climbing the world's tallest and most inaccessible peaks was ▮▮▮▮▮: the audience sat in rapt attention, the silence punctuated only by occasional gasps of amazement.

This is the end of the training session.
Read the explanations at the back. In the box below, note any words you came across that were unfamiliar, together with a meaning or an example of usage. Practice using these words with adults.

Word	A short sentence *you* have created, using the word

Matching Words

Identify which word is MOST SIMILAR in meaning to the word on the left. Each question has only one best answer. For each question shade your one chosen answer.

#	Word	cA⊃	cB⊃	cC⊃	cD⊃	cE⊃
1	**dogmatic**	inflexible	docile	canine	relevant	automated
2	**habitat**	pastime	decoration	shopping	design	environment
3	**guile**	cunning	overcoat	leather	muslin	yellowish
4	**doyen**	disciplinarian	deer	coinage	night-time	leader
5	**diminution**	delay	deposition	darkening	attenuation	dishevelment
6	**painstaking**	stabbing	agonising	multi-coloured	donating	meticulous
7	**repress**	replicate	overlay	interminable	subdue	publish

Opposite Words

Identify which word is MOST OPPOSITE in meaning to the word on the left. Each question has only one best answer. For each question shade your one chosen answer.

		⊂A⊃	⊂B⊃	⊂C⊃	⊂D⊃	⊂E⊃
8	**dawdled**	sketchy	accurate	hesitate	hasten	feared
9	**deplore**	admire	explore	implore	hesitate	resign

Words That Do Not Match

Identify which of the 5 options A-E matches LEAST WELL in meaning to the word on the left. There is only one best answer. Shade your one chosen answer.

		⊂A⊃	⊂B⊃	⊂C⊃	⊂D⊃	⊂E⊃
10	**vain**	overblown	inflated	proud	arrogant	valiant
11	**raucous**	rough	squawking	noisy	inharmonious	drunken

Odd One Out

Each group has four words which can have similar meanings, and one word which is different. Find the odd one out. Shade your one chosen answer.

	⊂A⊃	⊂B⊃	⊂C⊃	⊂D⊃	⊂E⊃
12	subtly	indirectly	obviously	tacitly	implicitly
13	strict	harsh	adamant	stern	ship

Go to the next page

14
    ⊂A⊃ sinuous   ⊂B⊃ sinful   ⊂C⊃ curving   ⊂D⊃ snaking   ⊂E⊃ twining

15
    ⊂A⊃ streak   ⊂B⊃ vein   ⊂C⊃ hint   ⊂D⊃ proud   ⊂E⊃ glint

16
    ⊂A⊃ torture   ⊂B⊃ persecute   ⊂C⊃ pester   ⊂D⊃ prosecute   ⊂E⊃ harass

17
    ⊂A⊃ wearing   ⊂B⊃ boring   ⊂C⊃ drilling   ⊂D⊃ monotonous   ⊂E⊃ dull

Find The Missing Letters

Complete the sentence by identifying the missing letters. Write one letter into each of the large boxes below. After writing each letter, shade its corresponding element in the A-Z block beside it.

18 "You can't make an om☐☐☐☐te without breaking eggs," pronounced David meaningfully as he shut off the lights during the protest meeting, triggering instant uproar.

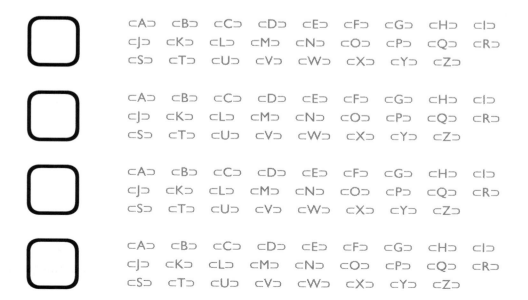

⊂A⊃ ⊂B⊃ ⊂C⊃ ⊂D⊃ ⊂E⊃ ⊂F⊃ ⊂G⊃ ⊂H⊃ ⊂I⊃
⊂J⊃ ⊂K⊃ ⊂L⊃ ⊂M⊃ ⊂N⊃ ⊂O⊃ ⊂P⊃ ⊂Q⊃ ⊂R⊃
⊂S⊃ ⊂T⊃ ⊂U⊃ ⊂V⊃ ⊂W⊃ ⊂X⊃ ⊂Y⊃ ⊂Z⊃

⊂A⊃ ⊂B⊃ ⊂C⊃ ⊂D⊃ ⊂E⊃ ⊂F⊃ ⊂G⊃ ⊂H⊃ ⊂I⊃
⊂J⊃ ⊂K⊃ ⊂L⊃ ⊂M⊃ ⊂N⊃ ⊂O⊃ ⊂P⊃ ⊂Q⊃ ⊂R⊃
⊂S⊃ ⊂T⊃ ⊂U⊃ ⊂V⊃ ⊂W⊃ ⊂X⊃ ⊂Y⊃ ⊂Z⊃

⊂A⊃ ⊂B⊃ ⊂C⊃ ⊂D⊃ ⊂E⊃ ⊂F⊃ ⊂G⊃ ⊂H⊃ ⊂I⊃
⊂J⊃ ⊂K⊃ ⊂L⊃ ⊂M⊃ ⊂N⊃ ⊂O⊃ ⊂P⊃ ⊂Q⊃ ⊂R⊃
⊂S⊃ ⊂T⊃ ⊂U⊃ ⊂V⊃ ⊂W⊃ ⊂X⊃ ⊂Y⊃ ⊂Z⊃

⊂A⊃ ⊂B⊃ ⊂C⊃ ⊂D⊃ ⊂E⊃ ⊂F⊃ ⊂G⊃ ⊂H⊃ ⊂I⊃
⊂J⊃ ⊂K⊃ ⊂L⊃ ⊂M⊃ ⊂N⊃ ⊂O⊃ ⊂P⊃ ⊂Q⊃ ⊂R⊃
⊂S⊃ ⊂T⊃ ⊂U⊃ ⊂V⊃ ⊂W⊃ ⊂X⊃ ⊂Y⊃ ⊂Z⊃

Similar relationships

Each sentence below states that one relationship is similar to another relationship. Choose the word, from options A to E, that completes the sentence best.

19

cAɔ	cBɔ	cCɔ	cDɔ	cEɔ
elongated	spindly	dishonest	hasty	old

Brevity is to concise as longevity is to ▮▮▮▮▮.

20

cAɔ	cBɔ	cCɔ	cDɔ	cEɔ
realise	chorus	dawn	midnight	daytime

Night is to dusk as morning is to ▮▮▮▮▮.

21

cAɔ	cBɔ	cCɔ	cDɔ	cEɔ
razzle	puddle	ignore	dimly	devastate

Darken is to dazzle as harken is to ▮▮▮▮▮.

Find The Missing Word

In each of the following pieces of text, one word is missing.
Complete it by choosing the one option A to E which fits best.

22

cAɔ	cBɔ	cCɔ	cDɔ	cEɔ
adept	addict	adapt	adroit	adopt

After some months of grumbling low-level protest, the sixth form finally agreed to ▮▮▮▮▮ the same uniform as the rest of the school.

23

cAɔ	cBɔ	cCɔ	cDɔ	cEɔ
distinct	distraught	distract	detained	distributed

Ant and Dec are in fact two ▮▮▮▮▮ people, even though they almost always work together.

Go to the next page ➡

24

cAɔ	cBɔ	cCɔ	cDɔ	cEɔ
illusion	excitation	allusion	collision	emulsion

We didn't at the time understand his ▮▮▮▮▮ to the need to sacrifice some minor freedoms. Only months later, from our prison cells, did his meaning become clear.

25

cAɔ	cBɔ	cCɔ	cDɔ	cEɔ
serial	serious	silted	cereal	spiral

The modern breakfast ▮▮▮▮▮ is supplemented with a variety of vitamins, which makes it very unlikely that a person with an average diet will become importantly deficient.

26

cAɔ	cBɔ	cCɔ	cDɔ	cEɔ
bone	brine	born	bore	borne

If you break any items in this museum, the cost must unfortunately be ▮▮▮▮▮ by your parents or your school.

27

cAɔ	cBɔ	cCɔ	cDɔ	cEɔ
novel	naval	snivel	never	navel

Even with the numbing effects of a long night of alcohol, he could not understand how he allowed himself to have his ▮▮▮▮▮ pierced.

28

cAɔ	cBɔ	cCɔ	cDɔ	cEɔ
despair	demure	despoil	demur	diminutive

In a complete contrast to Louisa who is loud and bold, her sister is soft-spoken and ▮▮▮▮▮.

29

cAɔ	cBɔ	cCɔ	cDɔ	cEɔ
chalet	caravan	piper	chaser	charlatan

We should have realised his potion would never work: in the last town where he performed his so-called faith healing, he was chased out as a ▬▬▬▬.

30

cAɔ	cBɔ	cCɔ	cDɔ	cEɔ
dissolution	embarkation	devastation	congregation	overdue

The end of the summer saw the ▬▬▬▬ of their hiking group, the members going their own ways.

This is the end of the training session.
Read the explanations at the back. In the box below, note any words you came across that were unfamiliar, together with a meaning or an example of usage. Practice using these words with adults.

Word	A short sentence *you* have created, using the word

Training Session 17

Matching Words

Identify which word is MOST SIMILAR in meaning to the word on the left. Each question has only one best answer. For each question shade your one chosen answer.

1 **recount**
- A analyse
- B describe
- C cumulate
- D error
- E photograph

2 **episodic**
- A uncomplicated
- B laughing
- C gripping
- D intermittent
- E continuous

3 **earnest**
- A wealthiest
- B closest
- C loudest
- D dedicated
- E funniest

4 **epoch**
- A earache
- B dog
- C lake
- D era
- E pocket

5 **gripe**
- A complaint
- B pudding
- C tubing
- D grasp
- E mature

6 **superfluous**
- A slithery
- B redundant
- C torrential
- D vivacious
- E pliable

7 **perturbed**
- A abbreviated
- B liquefied
- C scrawled
- D elongated
- E unsettled

Opposite Words

Identify which word is MOST OPPOSITE in meaning to the word on the left. Each question has only one best answer. For each question shade your one chosen answer.

		A	B	C	D	E
8	**disdain**	orientation	recognition	glee	cleanliness	health
9	**disband**	abandon	convene	silence	re-enable	relent

Words That Do Not Match

Identify which of the 5 options A-E matches LEAST WELL in meaning to the word on the left. There is only one best answer. Shade your one chosen answer.

		A	B	C	D	E
10	**retract**	withdraw	undo	renounce	announce	cancel
11	**revive**	uplift	resuscitate	revitalise	rouse	reactivate

Odd One Out

Each group has four words which can have similar meanings, and one word which is different. Find the odd one out. Shade your one chosen answer.

	A	B	C	D	E
12	piggish	swindler	trickster	fraudster	cheat
13	miser	twist	meander	coil	curve

Go to the next page

14

⊏A⊐	⊏B⊐	⊏C⊐	⊏D⊐	⊏E⊐
ravenous	sickly	morbid	unhealthy	diseased

15

⊏A⊐	⊏B⊐	⊏C⊐	⊏D⊐	⊏E⊐
confidence	self-esteem	spirit	morale	honest

16

⊏A⊐	⊏B⊐	⊏C⊐	⊏D⊐	⊏E⊐
cruel	mean	spittle	vengeful	spiteful

17

⊏A⊐	⊏B⊐	⊏C⊐	⊏D⊐	⊏E⊐
volatile	unstable	explosive	volcanic	lava

Find The Missing Letters

Complete the sentence by identifying the missing letters. Write one letter into each of the large boxes below. After writing each letter, shade its corresponding element in the A-Z block beside it.

18 Under the flickering fl☐☐☐☐scent light a tiny figure carrying a knapsack could just be made out, picking her way across the rubble towards the small huddle of emergency workers.

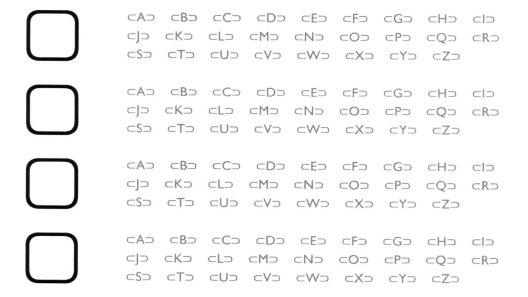

Similar relationships

Each sentence below states that one relationship is similar to another relationship. Choose the word, from options A to E, that completes the sentence best.

19
⊂A⊃	⊂B⊃	⊂C⊃	⊂D⊃	⊂E⊃
tub	murder	investigation	laughter	criminal

Butt is to joke as victim is to ▮▮▮▮▮▮ .

20
⊂A⊃	⊂B⊃	⊂C⊃	⊂D⊃	⊂E⊃
rude	bodybuilder	laughter	pimple	cheek

Bulge is to muscle as dimple is to ▮▮▮▮▮ .

21
⊂A⊃	⊂B⊃	⊂C⊃	⊂D⊃	⊂E⊃
tugging	inspire	lugging	spire	aspiring

Direction is to pointing as ambition is to ▮▮▮▮▮ .

Find The Missing Word

In each of the following pieces of text, one word is missing.
Complete it by choosing the one option A to E which fits best.

22
⊂A⊃	⊂B⊃	⊂C⊃	⊂D⊃	⊂E⊃
edited	affected	afflicted	effected	added

Dropping some of the money bags on the way, the gangsters ▮▮▮▮▮ a rapid getaway in the waiting car.

23
⊂A⊃	⊂B⊃	⊂C⊃	⊂D⊃	⊂E⊃
day	days	day's	days'	day's'

If you need to borrow a lawnmower, please give us three ▮▮▮▮▮ notice.

Go to the next page ➡

24

      ⊂A⊃   ⊂B⊃   ⊂C⊃   ⊂D⊃   ⊂E⊃
      gel   jibe   jelly   wobble   gibe

With every further ▮▮▮▮ like that, you do realise that your chances of being appointed prefect next year are decreasing, don't you?

25

      ⊂A⊃   ⊂B⊃   ⊂C⊃   ⊂D⊃   ⊂E⊃
      bugler   brother   burglar   birther   burger

If you leave that window unlocked, it is an open invitation to any passing ▮▮▮▮.

26

      ⊂A⊃   ⊂B⊃   ⊂C⊃   ⊂D⊃   ⊂E⊃
      bone   born   borne   brute   bought

By the time queen Clodagh gained the Northern lands, she had already ▮▮▮▮ her husband three fine, strapping sons.

27

      ⊂A⊃   ⊂B⊃   ⊂C⊃   ⊂D⊃   ⊂E⊃
      innocence   difference   humidity   deference   obligation

Whenever she enters the room in future, please make sure to show the appropriate level of ▮▮▮▮ for her leading role within our organisation.

28

      ⊂A⊃   ⊂B⊃   ⊂C⊃   ⊂D⊃   ⊂E⊃
      bridge   broach   brooch   breach   breech

It took half an hour of small talk and discussion of uncontroversial before I dared ▮▮▮▮ the real reason for my travelling to visit him in Frankfurt.

29

	cA⊃	cB⊃	cC⊃	cD⊃	cE⊃
	grisly	gristly	drizzling	grizzly	sizzling

Even in this magnificent restaurant, occasionally an expensive meat dish will have parts that are rather ███████.

30

	cA⊃	cB⊃	cC⊃	cD⊃	cE⊃
	renovate	coordinate	noticed	horrify	invigilate

Having heard of the shenanigans at last year's examination, the head master decided to personally ███████ at this year's examination.

This is the end of the training session.

Read the explanations at the back. In the box below, note any words you came across that were unfamiliar, together with a meaning or an example of usage. Practice using these words with adults.

Word	A short sentence *you* have created, using the word

1   C   seriousness

Gravity means either seriousness (associated with the adjective grave) or the force of attraction between massive objects across space. Attracting is not a noun.

2   D   calculation

A derivative is something based on something else, or a numerical value calculated from another set of numbers. It can also be used as an adjective to indicate the same concept of being based on something else.

3   C   spa

A resort is a place where people go for a holiday and for rest. A spa is a name for a resort involving water, or which is believed to directly improve health.

4   A   faint

Ethereal means very delicate and light. Originally, the ether was thought of as an imaginary thin matrix which was said to exist even in a vacuum.

5   C   recommend

To espouse has nothing to do with spouse. It means to recommend a course of action, a cause, a belief or a way of life.

6   A   remove

To extricate is to free someone or something from a difficult situation in which they are trapped; to remove them from such a problematic state.

7   A   perfect

Impeccable means fulfilling the highest standards, and being without any flaw. This word is often used to describe a high standard of manners or behaviour.

8   E   admit

To refuse to admit that something is true. Separately it can mean to refuse to give someone something or access to some facility (such as, for example, freedom).

9   C   fascinating

Drab means dull, uninteresting, lacklustre or (when describing a colour) a dull pale brown.

10   E   desk

A stable (noun) is a place that horses or other similar animals are housed. Stable (verb) means static, resistant to displacement, or reliable.

11   D   cubicle

To rectify means to put right (after making a mistake or misaligning something), or more generally to correct.

12   A   entombing

All the options are synonyms of captivating except entombing

13   A   mistake

All the options except mistake are synonyms for abate, which means weaken or subside, for example in a storm or dispute.

14   D   engrossing

All the options are synonyms of worthy except engrossing which means extremely interesting and capable of retaining attention.

15   A   exuberance

All the options are synonyms of vigilance except exuberance which means a very high degree of enthusiasm and excitement.

16   D   bare

All the other words can mean put up with, including bear. Bare is the odd one out: it means uncovered. Do not mix up bear and bare.

17   C   noisy

All the options are synonyms of vigorous except noisy .

18   'SENC': the word is 'absence'

Absence is the state of being away.

19   C   revealed

Maximised is a past tense verb, that means the opposite of decrease (a noun or verb). Look for a past tense verb that is opposite in meaning to obscure (which means to hide).

20   B   extra

Misnomer is a NOUN meaning a thing whose name is misleading. Apt is an ADJECTIVE meaning suitable. Since subtraction is a noun, look for an adjective.

21   A   helpful

In response to a death, other people are mournful. In response to someone in distress, other people are helpful. Funereal means resembling or relating to a funeral.

22   D   aloud

Aloud means spoken (rather than thought through mentally), while allowed means permitted. To allude is to refer to something.

23   B   effect

Effect (noun) means the change in something that is observed when something happens to it. The noun affect is in only rare use, denoting the visible features of their mood.

24   B   libel

Libel is a written statement knowingly making false claims in a manner that harms someone's reputation.

25   D   alternative

Alternative (noun or adjective) means a different option. The American use of the word "alternate" as an adjective resembling "alternative" is not considered correct British English.

26   B   digest

Digest means break down food into its constituent parts or, figuratively, process information by thinking. The noun can mean the results of digestion such as a summary of a long document.

27   E   desist

To desist is to stop doing something or trying to do something. In law it is used as part of "cease and desist", i.e. stop doing it now and don't just wait and try again shortly afterwards.

28   B   errand

An errand is a short journey undertaken to obtain or deliver something. The term is often used when the activity is done on behalf of someone else.

29   D   cajole

Cajole means persuade someone to do something by lengthy efforts which may include begging or flattery. While many of the options would fit in principle, only cajole fits the form of words.

30   A   torturous

Torturous means painful or horrible, like torture. In contrast, tortuous means only twisting and turning, with no implication of pain. The sentence indicates displeasure not twisting.

1   E   territory

A domain is an area controlled by or belonging to one authority or government. It can also refer to a field of knowledge in which a person is an expert.

2   E   apply

Exert means to make an effort, or to apply a force on something. To implicate is to say that someone was involved in, or was to blame for, something.

3   E   lasting

Enduring means continuing to exist for a long time, or to continuing to exist despite extremely adverse conditions.

4   B   definite

Emphatic means expressed strongly or unusually clearly. If someone asks for something emphatically, they are insisting upon it.

5   D   copy

Emulate means behave in the same way as, or copy. It can also mean follow the same path as someone else, for example in career or in pattern of marriage or divorce.

6   B   superfluous

Extraneous and superfluous both mean unnecessary, irrelevant to the subject being dealt with, or excess to requirements.

7   C   unintentionally

Inadvertently means without intending to do so; innocently, unintentionally, accidentally or unknowingly.

8   D   international

Domestic means in relation to a home or a family. Domestic also means something is about one country: this is in contrast to international, which means involving two or more countries.

9   A   grow

To ebb means to recede or decrease, and is used particularly to describe the tide withdrawing from high tide to low tide.

10   C   business

Customs are the usual habits of a place. A business might have one example of a culture, but they are not synonymous.

11   E   flight

A dilemma is a difficult situation, specifically facing a choice between two or more (usually unpleasant) options. A synonym is plight, but not flight.

12   B   gripping

Gripping means holding on to something; all the other words are synonyms of abrasive

13   E   circular

Circular is a specific shape; all the other words indicate wandering or extraordinariness and are synonyms of aberrant.

14   B   extracted

All the words are synonyms of absolute, except extracted which means removed or purified from something else.

15   E   dishonest
All the options are synonyms of vociferous except dishonest which means not telling the truth.

16   B   airborne
All the options are synonyms of volatile except airborne which means existing in the air, either as a traveller flying on a flight or a microbe or poison travelling through the air.

17   A   din
All the terms can relate to music, i.e. sounds that should be attractive or pleasant, except for din, which indicates an unpleasant or loud sound or continuous period of noise.

18   'USI': the word is 'business'
To help remember the spelling, think of "busy" and "ness", and just remember to change the "y" to an "i".

19   C   apoplectic
Apoplectic means in a state of extreme anger or rage. It is much more intense than annoyed. Similarly, being terrified is a much more intense feeling than being nervous.

20   B   overactive
Being impoverished (poor) is the result of being extravagant (spending money excessively and unwisely). Being exhausted is the result of excessive activity. Overactive is an adjective.

21   D   threat
One can be jealous of a possession, and fearful of a threat. Tip: if many options seem to fit, check whether only one fits the part of speech (noun/verb/adjective) or tense (for verbs).

22   E   naval
The A versus the E makes a big difference. Naval means in relation to a navy or ships. The navel is the umbilicus or belly-button.

23   E   declare
To declare is to publically state something, or to do it in a methodical and dignified way, or to make a statement to a tax authority.

24   C   continual
Continual is different from continuous. Continual means repeated episodes, presumably with gaps; continuous means a long period uninterrupted.

25   D   diminish
To diminish is to reduce or be made to appear smaller or less important. The object can be diminishing on its own, or something or someone can be diminishing it.

26   D   cursory
Cursory means superficial, excessively brief, or hasty. Discursive means a conversation or speech that is lengthy and has many digressions.

27   E   err
To err is to make a mistake (which can also be called an error). The question is a proverb, which means everybody makes mistakes, and we should try to forgive.

28   B   currant
A currant is a type of dried fruit, typically derived from grapes. It is used to stud currant buns, for example.

29   C   spurious
Spurious means fake or fabricated. In relation to an argument or form of reasoning, the word is used to indicate that it may seem reasonable but when analysed more deeply it is invalid or wrong.

30   E   perceptive
Perceptive means having the ability to notice things that are only slightly noticeable, or the ability to understand things with only a little information.

1 C prepare

To draft is to prepare a piece of writing. The term implies it is a first version which may be preliminary. In British English, the term that sounds like "draft" for a cool gust of air is "draught".

2 D hypnotise

Here it is important to recognise that entrance has two meanings, and the meaning being addressed here is the rarer one, namely the verb which means to put into a trance or a trance-like state.

3 C inconsistency

A discrepancy is a surprising lack of consistency between two facts; a conflict, mismatch or incompatibility.

4 B reflect

To ponder is to consider carefully and weigh up in one's mind. Synonyms: mediate, cogitate, ruminate, deliberate.

5 A amusing

Droll means amusing, especially if this is because of a subtle, unusual or curious feature. This is an old-fashioned word.

6 C disprove

To debunk is to prove something to be incorrect, or to be "bunkum", a term for nonsense. Synonyms are deflate, quash, expose, discredit, invalidate.

7 D saying

A proverb is a short saying that has passed down from ancient times, that conveniently expresses a concept. Typically the saying is a wise, concise summary of a complicated matter.

8 D income

An expense is the cost of doing or purchasing something: what has to be paid out in order to run a business.

9 A talkative

Dumb means unable or unwilling to speak: speechless. It does not mean stupid in British English. Excoriate means severely criticise someone.

10 E town

Facility can mean a place or arrangement of equipment that makes it possible to do something. Separately, it can mean a natural skill in doing something, such as a facility with languages.

11 B evening

Melancholy is a prolonged state of feeling sad; depression, gloom, pensiveness, sorrow, morning, downbeat, dispirited, dejected.

12 E relegate

Relegate means to be decreased in status, for example of a team being moved to a lower ranked grouping within a sport.

13 C fearsome

All the options are synonyms of witty except fearsome which means frightening.

14 C accurate

Dormant means asleep. It has special meanings derived from this. For animals, it can mean hibernation, i.e. deep sleep over winter. For volcanoes, it indicates the long time between eruptions.

15 E affluence

All the options are synonyms of veracity except affluence which means the state of being wealthy.

16 A composure

All the options are synonyms of vigour except composure which means the state of being cool, calm and collected.

17 D unified

All the options are synonyms of wholesome except unified which means made united, standardised or a single whole.

18 'EAS': the word is 'cease'

Cease is a somewhat formal word for stop. Separately, desist means do not start again.

19 E ordeal

Enjoy describes how one typically experiences a holiday. An ordeal is a painful, uncomfortable, embarrassing or difficult process. Endure is the best description of how one might experience an ordeal.

20 A nonchalant

Frozen is an adjective for the state opposite to searing (intense heating, surface burning). Look for an adjective for the state opposite to fascination. Nonchalant means showing no sign of interest.

21 E custom

Forthcoming describes an event in the future, such as an intention (something one plans to do). Bygone is an adjective describing something that happened in the past: custom is the most suitable noun.

22 D continuous

Continual is different from continuous. Continual means repeated episodes, presumably with gaps; continuous means a long period uninterrupted.

23 A birth

Birth means the process of being born, relating to a person, an animal, or a technique or process. A berth is a bunk or small room on a ship or boat.

24 C illusion

An illusion is a false appearance. It need not mean a deception, since it can occasionally arise naturally.

25 C alternate

Alternate (verb) means swap between one thing and another. Alternate (adjective) in the UK means every other one. For example, Mon/Wed/Fri versus Tue/Thu is a pattern of alternate days.

26 A boon

A boon is a gift, especially a prize given for a grand achievement.

27 A bizarre

Bizarre means very strange or unusual. A bazaar is a market, especially in the middle east.

28 D amiable

Amiable indicates that a person is friendly generally, but does not tell of a relationship between two people. In contrast "amicable" means a relationship that is friendly and lacking dispute.

29 A lamented

To lament is to express sorrow, sadness or grief in an intensely emotional way. Synonyms: grieve, groan, moan, wail, cry, sob, howl.

30 D digression

A digression is a sidestep onto a different matter, occurring during a conversation, lecture or piece of writing. It is implied that the main subject will be returned to.

1   C   residue

A deposit (noun) is money paid in to an account, or as a partial pre-payment for a purchase. It can also mean anything left behind after everything else has moved on. There is an equivalent verb.

2   E   doorway

Entrance (noun, accent on "en") means a place of entry. Entrance (verb, accent on "trance") means to put into a trance. Inflow is flow of fluid into something.

3   E   elaborate

Extravagant means unrestrained in spending or resource utilisation, greatly in excess of what is reasonable for the purpose.

4   D   flirtatious

Coy means pretending to be shy, but in reality intending to cause attraction. It can also mean evasive, when applied to an answer to a question.

5   B   conscientious

Dutiful means careful to fulfil one's duty; conscientious. It also suggests the activity is because of a sense of responsibility rather than exciting or attractive for the person.

6   E   sacrilege

Desecration is the act of damaging or using incorrectly something which is holy or sacred to a religion or to the cultural beliefs of certain people.

7   A   storyteller

A raconteur is someone who can tell stories in an interesting manner, and whom people enjoy listening to. The word is related to the French word for recount.

8   E   hesitant

Decisive (of a person) means being able to reach a decision quickly, or (of a fact or a piece of information) able to resolve a question or dispute.

9   E   hide

Exhibit means display openly, either a characteristic (skill or quality) or an item of art (such as in an art gallery or museum).

10   C   pathway

Extract (verb) means to pull out, or to determine by a process of logic, or copy (and perhaps summarise). In chemistry, it can mean purify. It can mean to obtain from someone by threat or force.

11   D   complex

To be complicit in something is to be part of a group that plans to do that thing. Typically the thing is illegal or immoral. One can be complicit by actively doing something or by knowingly remaining silent.

12   A   implicate

Implicate is to suggest blame should be placed on someone; the other words indicate the design or creation of a plan.

13   B   persuasive

All the options are synonyms of widespread except persuasive which means able to persuade or convince someone.

14   A   extinguished

All the words are synonyms of absorbed, except extinguish which means (of a fire or light) put out or ended.

15 C disconsolate

Disconsolate means extremely sad; the other words are synonyms for something that is very bad.

16 A undermined

All the options are synonyms of wretched except undermined which means reduce the power or status of a person, especially if done secretly and gradually.

17 D opaque

All the options are synonyms of vindicate except opaque which means impossible to see through.

18 'HAME': the word is 'chameleon'

A chameleon is an animal that changes its colour to suit its surroundings.

19 E wrist

A ring is an item of jewellery that is slipped over a finger. Likewise a bracelet is an item of jewellery that is worn around the wrist.

20 D legs

Unlike a line segment, a circle has no ends. Therefore look for something a snake does not have: legs. It is true that not all snakes bite, but some snakes do bite while no snakes have legs.

21 D boil

Contrition (noun) is being sorry for what one has done wrong; to deny (verb) is to say one didn't even do it. Boil is the verb most near opposite meaning to refrigerate.

22 E credibility

Credibility is the ability of people in general to believe the person or thing being described.

23 B break

To break is to snap into two (or more) pieces, or to pause a meeting. A brake is a system in a car that keeps it stationary when parked, or slow it down when driving.

24 E ego

The ego is the conscious self. The word is commonly used to mean one's sense of self-importance. Sometimes the word is used to mean an excessive self-importance.

25 C delusion

A delusion is a false, unshakeable belief, that is not the result of being part of a group (such a football team or religion).

26 C sensor

A sensor is a device for sensing or detecting things.

27 D cache

Cash is money in the form of notes and coins (as opposed to cheques or credit cards). A cache is a secret store of items.

28 A ambiguous

Ambiguous means having two (or more) interpretations or meanings. In the case described, one triangle could turn into the other in two different ways, so it is not possible to find out which way is correct.

29 E tortuous

Tortuous means twisting and turning. It does not mean like torture: that is torturous. We can tell the writer did not find twists and turns painful because he or she said it was enjoyable.

30 E repudiate

To repudiate is to reject an allegation, agreement or policy; to say it is not valid, not appropriate or not true.

1 E volume

Capacity means ability or (in relation to a chamber or vessel) the internal size or volume. It can similarly mean the quantity that someone or something can do, such as a production capacity.

2 B code

An ethic is a set of principles by which someone lives or works. For example, a work ethic is a habit of working hard.

3 C wandering

Erratic means irregular and unpredictable in pattern or movement; wandering or random. If used to describe a person, it indicates that person is unreliable or untrustworthy.

4 E nurture

Cultivate means carefully work to help plants grow, or work on the soil to prepare it for planting, or work on developing a skill, or carefully and intentionally develop a friendship with someone.

5 E amenable

Docile means peaceful, soft, submissive or willing to accept instruction or control. It suggests that the person can be easily manipulated or made to do things.

6 B distasteful

Repugnant means extremely unacceptable, especially if it is on grounds of taste or decency. It has a rarer meaning of "in conflict with".

7 E terrible

Insufferable means so awful or extreme that it cannot be tolerated, such as an insufferable bore. When used to describe a person (without specifying why) it means extremely arrogant.

8 B taciturn

Loquacious means tending to talk a lot. Taciturn means very quiet. Both terms tend to apply to a person's behaviour in the long term.

9 E inside

Inside, as a noun, can mean the interior of an object: "the inside of the house was as clean as the outside."

10 C export

Foreign means relating to a different country, or the language of a different country. It can also mean unfamiliar or alien.

11 D affluent

Incongruous means not in keeping with other nearby items or the general environment. Synonyms are inappropriate, unsuitable, out of keeping, out of place.

12 A compromise

All the options are synonyms of wither except compromise which means (of a negotiation) an agreement achieved by each side giving in a little.

13 C amateur

All the options are synonyms of expert or virtuoso except amateur which implies beginner or not professional.

14 C virtual

All the options are synonyms of virulent except virtual.

15 B helpful
All the options are synonyms of woeful except helpful.

16 A conical
All the options are synonyms of viable except conical which means shaped like a cone.

17 C diminished
All the options are synonyms of wistful except diminished which means reduced.

18 'HRON': the word is 'chronicle'
A chronicle is a log of events, laid out in order of time.

19 B bird
A hoof is the extremity of the leg of a horse. In the same way, a claw is the extremity of the lower limb of a bird. (A talon is a synonym for claw)

20 D Canada
The eagle is a creature symbolic of America. The moose is similarly a creature symbolic of Canada.

21 C burn
To dislocate (e.g. a shoulder) is to move in a particular way that is harmful. Likewise to burn is to give warmth in a particular way and intensity that is harmful.

22 D wave
Wave means to move one's hand or a flag. As a noun, a wave can be a sudden surge of distress or emotion, or a movement of water surfaces. Waive means set aside one's normal right to demand something.

23 E accept
Accept means to receive. Except means to exclude.

24 D lofty
Lofty means very high, or (figuratively) of a high intellectual, moral or cultural standard, or (of a person) withdrawn or aloof, perhaps due to an exaggerated sense of self-worth.

25 E celestial
Celestial means relating to the heavens, or astronomy. Saturnine does not mean relating to Saturn: it means (of a person) that they are gloomy generally.

26 A callous
Callous means cruel but predominantly in the sense of being uncaring rather than enjoying causing harm.

27 E defuse
Defuse is to inactivate the trigger mechanism of a bomb or, by analogy, reduce the level of aggression in an argument. Diffuse (adjective or verb) means spread over a large area.

28 B cryptic
Cryptic means encoded. This word is used to describe crosswords where the clues are deliberately difficult, or more generally where information is encoded to make it more difficult to understand.

29 E altogether
It must start with a vowel, because of the "an". Altogether means completely or having totalled up everything. All together are two separate words indicating coming together, but not a calculation.

30 D tantamount
Tantamount means equivalent to, or as bad as.

1   C   teaching

A policy or set of traditional beliefs taught by a religious organisation, government, pressure group or political party.

2   E   slippery

Elusive means difficult to locate, capture or achieve. The term can also be used for thoughts that are hard to pin down.

3   D   clear

Lucid means easy to understand, clear and plain. Lurid is an adjective used to describe details, crimes, events, or accusations that are disgusting, agonising and horrific.

4   D   mourn

To grieve is to mourn for the loss of someone. A greave is a shinguard. A groove is a narrow valley-shaped depression in a structure.

5   C   trapped

To embroil is to involve someone deeply into a conflict or argument, or other form of difficult situation that consumes their attention, time or focus.

6   D   perfect

Exquisite means delicate or extremely beautiful. In another meaning it indicates a sensation that is unusually powerful, such as pain, joy or love.

7   A   disorderly

Slovenly means untidy or dirty, careless or with poor attention to detail. Synonyms: slapdash, slipshod, lackadaisical, slack, lax, negligent, haphazard, unmethodical.

8   C   concentrated

Diluted means spread out thinly or having had other material (typically another liquid) added to reduce its concentration.

9   E   honesty

Duplicity is the habit of being dishonest.

10   D   overburden

Elaborate (adjective) means detailed and complicated. Elaborate (verb) means lay out in detail, for example in relation to plans.

11   D   fascination

Notoriety is fame for something extraordinarily bad; similar to infamy. Synonyms are: disrepute, opprobrium, dishonour.

12   C   indicative

All the options are synonyms of vindictive except indicative.

13   A   frantic

All the options are synonyms of zealot except frantic which means overcome with emotion, especially if this is anxiety or fear.

14   A   ewe

Ewe means a female sheep. All the others are words for male members of a species.

15   D   corrosion

All the words mean bad behaviour of people: cheating or doing immoral acts as individuals or as a group. Corrosion means rusting.

16   D   delicious

All the options are synonyms of vitriolic except delicious which means extremely tasty or beautiful.

17   B   convey

All the options mean to say that something is bad or of poor quality, except for convey which means to carry, take or send something somewhere.

18   'ECEI': the word is 'deceive'

Deceive means put a lie into someone's head, either by telling a lie or giving (or allowing them to fall into) a false impression in some other way.

19   A   wheels

A table is supported by legs. For a truck, the corresponding items that support it are the wheels.

20   C   guitar

One uses a broom to sweep, and a guitar to strum. (One can indeed tune a guitar, but cannot sweep a broom.)

21   B   fire

If you add water, you stop something being concentrated (i.e. you dilute it). The thing you can add to stop something being cold is fire.

22   B   bow

The bow of the ship is its front section. To bow is to bend forward in a formal greeting. A bow is a curved, typically wooden, stringed weapon for firing arrows. A bough is a branch of a tree.

23   E   decline

Decline means reject an offer. In grammar, it is a description of the process of changing a word to represent different grammatical uses within a language.

24   B   lodge

Lodge (verb) means formally place or register. Lodge (noun) is a house or hotel, typically in the countryside or forest; or a group within some types of club or society, for example, Freemasons.

25   C   chord

 A chord is a group of musical notes that are played together to produce a pleasant sound. A cord is a piece of string or a biological part that resembles a piece of string.

26   D   burden

Burden means load. It can refer to a thing being physically carried, or a mental load.

27   C   adverse

Adverse means having a harmful effect. Averse describes the opinion of a person who is against a concept. Avers is a present tense of the verb aver, which means to insist that something is true.

28   C   levity

Levity is lightheartedness, cheeriness or humour, particularly when relating to a matter that in reality should be handled with seriousness and dignity.

29   E   culpable

Culpable means deserving of blame or criticism. This word is used when someone or something is harmed, and the speaker wants to state that the fault lies with someone in particular.

30   B   lethargic

Lethargic means moving slowly, feeling tired and unenergetic, and perhaps sleepy.

1 C argument

To debate is to challenge or dispute something. A debate (noun) is a process involving such a dispute.

2 A meet

Encounter means meet, with an accent on the meeting being not planned. It can be with a person, event or challenge.

3 D approve

To endorse can mean to approve something (for example, a project or an expenditure). Alternatively it can mean make a note on the back of a cheque that alters the way it is paid.

4 C swarm

A horde is a large group of creatures that are moving together, or a crowd of people. Synonyms are: herd (animals), or mob or throng (people).

5 E illogical

Fallacious means based on incorrect logic (reasoning) or based on an incorrect fact. In either case, if you say something is fallacious you are saying the conclusion is incorrect.

6 A copiousness

Copiousness means in large quantities, or in far more than sufficient supply. It can refer to items that are counted, or to liquids that have volume.

7 A devoted

Loyal means giving consistent support or assistance to a cause, an organisation or a person.

8 C implied

Explicit means indicated clearly, rather than only in a subtle way.

9 D damnation

An eulogy is a speech in praise of someone, most commonly at a funeral when the person has died.

10 D complete

Endure means to suffer something unpleasant, or to continue to exist for a long time, especially in difficult or unpleasant conditions.

11 E demonstrate

To deprecate is to express disapproval of something, most commonly a behaviour. Synonyms: denounce, deplore, oppose.

12 E perspire

All the words mean to devise a plan to do something, probably illegal or immoral, in a cunning way. Connive and conspire indicate more than one person is involved. Perspire means sweat.

13 D impish

Impish means mischievous or naughty, whereas all the other words mean a supply that is very limited or insufficient.

14 E mislaid

All the options can mean something is imaginary, erroneous or made up, except mislaid which means something has been lost.

15   E   peer

They all mean the top of something, except peer which means to look into something carefully, with difficulty or without being noticed.

16   B   peak

They all mean look at something (with difficulty or with concentration) except peak which is the top of something.

17   A   temperature

They all mean intense enthusiasm, feeling or passion (synonyms: zest, vigour, spirit, avidity) except for temperature.

18   'ICC': the word is 'desiccate'

The spelling is desiccate, with one S and two Cs.

19   E   gallon

A metre is a metric (SI unit) measure of distance, while inch is a non-metric measure of distance. A non-metric measure of volume is gallon.

20   D   machines

A shop sells wares (items for sale) that people want. Similarly an inventor makes machines that do something useful.

21   A   network

We use a browser to make contact across the internet. We use a telephone to make contact across a telephone network.

22   A   course

Course means a direction or route followed by a vehicle or boat (or road or river), or part of a meal. As a verb it can mean to flow rapidly or chase in a blood sport).

23   B   council

A council is a group of people, whereas to counsel (with an S and an E) is to give advise.

24   A   assent

Assent (noun) means approval for something, and the corresponding verb means to give such approval. Ascent is the process of ascending (climbing up) something.

25   C   diffuse

Diffuse (adjective or verb) means spread over a large area rather than entirely focused on one point. Defuse is to inactivate the trigger mechanism of a bomb or reduce the aggression in an argument.

26   B   advise

Advise is the verb; advice is the noun.

27   B   bough

A bough is a branch of a tree. Bow can mean (noun) a weapon used for firing arrows, or the front of a ship or (verb) the act of tilting the head and/or body forward in a formal greeting.

28   A   coax

Coax means get someone to do something by patient encouragement and persuasion.

29   A   irritate

Irritate means make someone annoyed, or cause inflammation or damage in the body. Aggravate means make worse a situation that is already bad, or accentuate an existing injury. (One cannot aggravate a person.)

30   C   demeanour

Demeanour is an aspect of a person's appearance that tells us about the state of mind of that person.

1 E ghastly

Lurid is an adjective used to describe details, crimes, events, or accusations that are disgusting, agonising and horrific. Lucid means easy to understand, clear and plain.

2 A condolence

Commiseration is compassion, condolence or sympathy for what others are suffering. For example, "I offer my commiserations to my competitor whom I just managed to pip to the post."

3 B portray

To depict is to draw or paint or sculpt something that represents something else; figuratively it can be used for a description of something conveyed in any manner, including words or mime.

4 B desire

A craving is an intense desire, especially if the feeling is unusual for the person. For example, during pregnancy, a woman may crave foods she does not normally particularly like.

5 D delete

To expunge is to remove completely and utterly; to thoroughly obliterate and remove all trace of something.

6 E sacred

Hallowed means revered or sacred. It is related to the word "holy". Hollowed means gouged out. For example, a canoe can be made by hollowing out a log.

7 A project

To extrapolate is to project beyond the information one already has, to times or positions beyond those. For example, one might project previous price trends for an item to predict a future price.

8 A clear

Ambiguous means having conflicting interpretations, especially when it is an instruction that cannot therefore cannot be followed. It does not mean indecision. Ambivalent means being unable to decide.

9 C curse

A euphemism is a special polite or indirect way of saying something that softens the impact of hearing about it.

10 C character

Caricature means to draw (or describe) someone in a simplistic way which exaggerates key characteristics, often specifically to mock them.

11 A metallic

Mercurial describes a person who has a habit of suddenly changing their mind, or switching between interests, without apparent reason.

12 E control

They can all have a similar meaning, i.e. withstanding a difficult condition, environment, treatment or punishment, except control.

13 D mutate

All the words can mean die, except mutate which means change. Mutation in biology means a sudden change of features from one generation to the next.

14 C collect

They all mean to undo a policy, order or instruction, except for collect. Repeal is particularly used for laws; retract for publications; countermand for orders.

15   C   gregarious

All the words are synonym of aggregate (bring together) except for gregarious which means a person who likes to get together.

16   A   repair

All can be synonyms of receive. For example, one can receive surgery or undergo surgery. The exception is repair.

17   D   hostile

All the words are synonyms of significant or important, except for hostile which means the state of being an enemy.

18   'LLIE': the word is 'ebullient'

Ebullient means very cheerful and energetic; giving off this energy to others.

19   A   type

One uses a computer mouse to point to things, and a computer keyboard to type things.

20   C   throw

A card can be played, to derive entertainment. Likewise, a ball can be thrown for entertainment.

21   D   face

A vertex is the place where two edges meet. An edge, in turn, is the place where two faces meet.

22   E   box

Box, in this sense, means impose limits. Constrain has a similar meaning but the word needs to fit "# you in", which box, but not constrain, can do.

23   E   capital

The capital is the main or leading city of a country. A capital is an upper case letter, such as "A", in contrast to the lower case "a". Capital (adjective) means major or relating to the head.

24   B   aisle

An aisle is a central walking space between two sides of seats (in a theatre or church) or items for sale (in a supermarket). An isle is a small island. To ail is to be ill or become ill.

25   C   flounder

Flounder means walk in a disorganised manner through obstacles, e.g. through water, or have difficulty with a task. Founder means (as a noun) the person who started something or (of a ship) to sink.

26   A   adapt

Adapt is to modify and (only then) use a thing. Adopt is simply to take into one's possession, or set of habits, a thing or habit from somewhere or someone else.

27   D   bridal

Bridal means relating to a bride. A bridle is an arrangement of straps surrounding a horse's head.

28   B   bazaar

A bazaar is a marketplace. The term originated in the Middle East. Bizarre means very unusual or abnormal.

29   E   afflicted

Afflicted means that someone is suffering from an influence, e.g. a disease, or disability. Inflicted means delivered a damaging blow to someone, either physically or figuratively (through words).

30   E   barmy

Barmy is an informal term indicating crazy or mad. Balmy refers to weather that is pleasantly warm.

1 C quack

A quack is a person claiming to have medical skill or knowledge, but who does not. A sham is a fake person or thing.

2 B evade

To elude is to escape from someone or something that is chasing or causing danger. It suggests the escape is clever rather than merely chance. It can also describe a skill that one temporarily loses.

3 A demanding

Exacting means setting or requiring high standards of skill or achievement. For example, one might have an exacting teacher; building a computer is an exacting task.

4 A ridicule

To deride is to make fun of something, or indicate that it is worthless or laughable. Synonyms are ridicule, mock, jibe at, pillory, jeer at, scoff at.

5 D complete

Exhaustive means thorough, complete and comprehensive, missing nothing. It is different from exhaustING which means tiring.

6 D credulous

Gullible means able to be gulled; gulled is an old word for tricked. Credulous means trusting. Amphibious means able to live in both water and land.

7 B wise

Sagacious means wise, like a sage; showing good judgement, fairness, foresight, thoughtfulness or shrewdness.

8 E correct

Erroneous means in error, or incorrect.

9 A fail

To excel is to be outstandingly good at doing or knowing about something.

10 A upstairs

Elated means very happy indeed. Synonyms: overjoyed, gleeful, excited, animated, jubilant, ecstatic, euphoric.

11 D amateur

Amateur means a beginner; all the other words mean experienced or skilful.

12 D colloquial

All can mean very generous with words, deeds or money, except for colloquial which means the type of language used by a common person rather than formally correct language.

13 E cleanse

All the words mean fight back or reject (parry is used in sword fighting or debating) except cleanse which is to make clean.

14 B efficiency

All the words mean a lack of something (in the case of drought, it is rain) except for efficiency, which means the ability or habit of doing something quickly, easily and using few resources.

15   D   liquefy

All the words mean give up something (in the case of abdicate, it is giving up the status of being king or queen), except liquefy which means turn from solid to liquid.

16   D   secretive

All the words mean optional, not essential, open to free choice. The exception is secretive which means done in secret or (of a person) having a habit of doing things secretly.

17   B   invalid

Invalidate would mean the same as the others, which all mean to cancel or undo a previous action or state. However invalid is an adjective or a noun meaning incorrect or sick.

18   'IGHT': the word is 'eighth'

One divided by eight is one eighth. The key to the spelling is to first write eight, and then add an "h".

19   E   handle

One operates a button by pressing it. Typically, one operates a handle by turning it.

20   C   tablet

One would write on paper, and chisel a tablet (of stone or wood).

21   A   water

An omelette is made of egg. A cloud is made of water (in the form of tiny water droplets light enough to float in the air).

22   C   brake

A brake is a device to keep a vehicle stationary. A break is a gap, pause or division into two parts.

23   C   curb

To curb is to limit something. A kerb is a pavement or the stone edging of a pavement or path.

24   B   clause

A clause is a part of a sentence. In legal terms, this term is used to indicate one of a series of items in, for example, a law or contract.

25   B   despair

To despair is to completely lose hope. The noun despair describes the state of having completely lost hope.

26   A   detached

Detached means not physically connected (attached) to something. In relation to a person, it indicates that they are withdrawn or aloof.

27   C   allude

Allude means mention, directly or indirectly. Elude means successfully escape. Étude is derived the French and means study. In English it is applied to a short musical training piece.

28   D   cynicism

Cynicism is the belief that everyone is motivated by selfishness rather than the desire to make the world better or to be honourable.

29   E   credulous

Credulous means having an intense capacity to believe or trust, even in things that should be easily recognised as untrue. This is description of a person, and not of the thing being believed.

30   B   brusque

Brusque means abrupt or brief to a degree that might be rude; to some extent it indicates some degree of disrespect.

1   C   articulacy

Eloquence means persuasive speaking or writing, or skilful use of language. Synonyms are oratory (for speaking), rhetoric, and grandiloquence.

2   A   lie

A deceit is a lie, an untrue statement presented as though it was true. Deceit is also the practice of telling such lies.

3   C   fizzy

Effervescent means a liquid or drink which is fizzy; by extension it is applied to people who are enthusiastic and fun-loving.

4   B   corrupt

Venial and venal are easily confused. Venial (with an I) means minor, whereas venal means susceptible to bribery.

5   D   hugeness

Enormity means very great size, seriousness or importance. The word is derived from enormous. It particularly relates to things that are bad, evil or criminal.

6   B   neutral

Indifferent has two meanings. It can mean uninterested or unconcerned. Alternatively it can mean neither good nor bad, i.e. neutral.

7   A   scheme

To machinate is to plot or scheme, most commonly in secret, to achieve some future aim. The word suggests this activity is clever and probably for an evil purpose.

8   D   glut

A dearth is a shortage or lack of something. A glut is an excess of something.

9   A   inspire

Exhale means breathe out (expire). Inhale (or inspire) means breathe in.

10   D   acidic

Dour is a term applied to a person to indicate they have a general tendency to be hard, unfriendly, pessimistic and severe.

11   A   intelligible

Contemptible means worthy of contempt, because it is so awful, illegal or otherwise ghastly. Some synonyms are: hateful, detestable, reprehensible, loathsome, odious, revolting.

12   C   countryside

All the other words mean attractive to look at. They may be used in relationship to a countryside but they are not synonymous.

13   C   versatile

Versatile means able to do many different things well. The other words are to do with good or honourable behaviour.

14   A   pretty

Other than pretty, all the words mean something occurring quickly, without a gradual onset.

15   B   storm

Other than storm, all the other words mean to annoy.

16   A   subtract

Other than subtract, all the other words are ways of describing what something is made of.

17   E   adjective

An adjective is a word describing a noun. The other words indicate things are side-by-side and touching.

18   'HILA': the word is 'exhilarating'

Exhilarating means thrilling. If you are exhilarated you are very happy and elated, highly energised.

19   C   circle

Distorting a square by stretching it in one direction produces an oblong rectangle. Doing the same to a circle produces an ellipse.

20   D   music

A screen is the device that enables you to observe a picture. Likewise, a loudspeaker is a device that enables you to hear music.

21   B   berthing

At an airport, craft are landing to bring in passengers. At a marina, ships are berthing (being moored) to bring in passengers.

22   B   along

A long and along are different. Along is a preposition indicating movement in a continuous trajectory, or arranged in an approximately horizontally pattern in association with something else.

23   C   liberty

Liberty is freedom, either in the sense of not being in prison, or in the sense of being unrestricted in choice in general.

24   E   category

Category means class or division of things or people, based on shared characteristics

25   B   founder

Founder means (as a noun) the person who sets up an enterprise or (as a verb applied to a ship) to sink. This is unrelated to flounder which means to walk in a disorganised manner through obstacles.

26   A   brooch

A brooch is a piece of jewellery worn by attachment to an upper garment such as a blouse. To broach is to open discussion of a subject, or to break down a wall or barrier.

27   B   coherent

Coherent means fitting or sticking together. It can refer to an argument being consistent and logical, or to anything that fits together into a unified whole.

28   A   haddock

Haddock is a type of sea fish, related to cod.

29   C   aggravate

Aggravate means do something to make a problem, crime or adverse situation worse. It is distinct from irritate, which does not indicate that the problem was present before.

30   A   braggart

A braggart is someone who boasts or brags about what they have done, their abilities or what they own.

1   C   being

Entity means a thing such as a business, country or region of a country, or a creature (to identify it as a single creature, even though its boundaries may be unclear).

2   E   puzzle

An enigma is something mysterious and difficult to properly understand; an extremely challenging puzzle.

3   B   focus

Emphasis means the stress applied to certain words in speech to indicate their importance, or in general the importance of some things.

4   E   minor

Venial and venal are easily confused. Venial (with an l) means minor, whereas venal means susceptible to bribery.

5   B   shout

To exclaim is to cry out or shout suddenly, indicating pain, strong (positive or negative) emotion or surprise.

6   D   unbeatable

Indomitable means very resistant to being defeated or subdued. It is commonly used in the phrase "indomitable spirit", meaning a courageous character.

7   C   weaken

To debilitate is to reduce someone's ability, by making them disabled or weakened. An antonym would be rehabilitate.

8   A   promote

To promote is to recommend something or someone, or to increase its value or status. To discredit is to reduce people's respect or trust in a person or thing.

9   D   assist

Hamper means to impair, impeded, obstruct or delay. It has an unrelated meaning, as a noun, of a basket, especially of food, for example for a picnic.

10   B   scream

Eke means be frugal with limited resources so that they last longer. It also means to survive in circumstances made difficult by lack of resources.

11   C   cost-efficient

Spendthrift (noun or adjective) means a person who spends money carelessly or wastefully. Synonyms: profligate, prodigal, irresponsible.

12   E   haggle

Bargain, in the sense in which it matches the other words, is a settled agreement (not the process of haggling to reach it).

13   C   advertise

Advertise means increase public awareness of something. All the other words refer to a disastrous or argumentative meeting.

14   B   pickle

All the words refer to someone who has a habit of changing their mind without necessarily having a reason, except pickle.

15   D   clementine

A clementine is a fruit and nothing to do with the others. Clandestine, like the other words, means secretive or like a spy.

16   E   sensible

Other than sensible, all the other words indicate cleanliness and freedom from dirt or infection.

17   D   flaunt

To flaunt is to show something off to the degree that others think the behaviour rude. To flout is to openly break a law or rule.

18   'IEF': the word is 'grief'

Tip: When you know that there is a sound of "EE" made up of an I and an E, and you don't know the order, the rule is "I before E except after C". A notable exception is seize.

19   A   carrot

Alcohol and tea are both liquids that are drunk. Cake and carrot are both solid foods that are eaten.

20   C   ill

If comedy is successful, it will make you no longer sad. If medicine is successful, it will make you no longer ill.

21   C   thaw

A printer converts electronic information into paper form; a scanner does the reverse. To thaw is the reverse of to freeze.

22   C   brief

Brief, in this sense, means give information to. The speaker is asking someone to come and join him or her urgently, and promises to explain the reason when the listener arrives.

23   C   advice

Advice is the noun; advise is the verb. TIP: Advice is uncountable, like peace. If you give advice and then later again give advice, these are not two "advices" but instead two pieces of advice.

24   E   affect

When used as verbs, affect and effect have the following meanings. Affect means change something, give a false impression, or to create an effect (noun). Effect (verb) means to achieve something.

25   B   averse

Averse means having one's mind set against something. Adverse means interfering with or obstructing the achievement of something.

26   A   despot

A despot is a ruler who has total power in a country. This word is used especially if such a ruler uses this power in a cruel, vicious or brutal way.

27   D   deduce

Deduce means determine by a logical process, most commonly by excluding all the other possibilities.

28   A   engender

Engender means to influence people in a way that creates an effect. For example, a controversial lecture can engender extensive discussion amongst the audience.

29   C   spontaneity

Spontaneity means without elaborate pre-planning; resulting from impulse thoughts at the last minute. It can also be used to indicate independence from external influence.

30   B   dissemble

Dissemble means to tell lies. Do not confuse this with disassemble which means to separate into component parts.

1   B   assist

To facilitate is to assist, accelerate or otherwise make a process happen with less difficulty than would otherwise be the case.

2   C   ambiguous

Equivocal means allowing the possibility of several meanings (i.e. Ambiguous) or unclear. The term can be used to describe advice that is unhelpful or a test whose result cannot be interpreted clearly.

3   E   uncertain

Dubious means suspected of being incorrect. It is the suspicion that is the focus. If it was known to be definitely incorrect, it would not be dubious.

4   C   scholarly

Erudite means relating to a high level of sophistication and scholarship.

5   E   list

Enumerate means to list a series of things, one by one. Historically, it also was used to mean simply count them.

6   A   reluctance

Disinclination is lack of keenness to do something, and a mild reluctance to do it. Other synonyms are unwillingness, indisposition, and hesitancy.

7   B   support

To corroborate is to obtain information from another source which confirms what the first source is saying; to confirm from independent information.

8   E   evolve

To degenerate is to become worse; to evolve is to change over time with an implication that this is an improvement.

9   B   friendship

Enmity is the feeling of intense dislike or hatred, such as between two people who are enemies.

10   D   vegetable

Pliant means flexible. When applied to people, it indicates that the person is willing to accept the decisions, actions or preferences of others. It is nothing to do with "plant".

11   D   discover

All the words are synonyms of research, except discover which is what may happen at the end of such a process.

12   A   simplistic

Simplistic is not a good thing to be: it means oversimplified, missing important details and perhaps misunderstanding the whole matter being addressed.

13   A   flout

To flaunt is to show something off to the degree that others think the behaviour rude. To flout is to openly break a law or rule.

14   D   embarrassed

All the words mean careful with money, except embarrassed.

15   E   pom-pom

A pom-pom is a fluffy decoration that is used for waving during celebrations or displays. The other words refer to a person with an exaggerated sense of their own worth.

16   C   persecute

Prosecute/Persecute. Prosecute means to take someone to court, accusing them of having committed a crime. This is different from persecute, which is an illegal act of suppressing a person or group.

17   D   confuse

All the words are forms of suffering, except confuse.

18   'RIEV': the word is 'grievance'

A grievance is a feeling that one has cause for complaint especially because of receiving bad treatment. Tip: For the "EE" sound made up of an I and an E, the rule is "I before E except after C".

19   C   downpour

The purpose of a seatbelt is to give protection in the event of a collision (car crash). The purpose of an umbrella is to give protection in the event of a downpour.

20   B   breaking

The purpose of a castle is to defend what is inside. The destruction of a castle is an ultimate form of failure. Likewise the breaking of a promise is an ultimate form of failure.

21   D   damage

To publicise is a verb in the infinitive form ("to ....") for the process of making something not secret. Likewise to damage is a verb in the infinitive form for making something not protected.

22   D   altar

An altar is a table or similar surface used in religious ceremonies, especially Christian.

23   C   affected

Affected can be a past tense verb meaning changed or influenced, but also has a different meaning of artificial, insincere or faked, when applied to a person's behaviour or apparent disability.

24   E   bridle

A bridle is the strapping, often leather, around a horse's head. To bridle means to apply a bridle, or, figuratively, to suddenly protest when asked to do something. Bridal means relating to a bride.

25   B   waive

Waive, with an I, means set aside one's right to something. Wave means move a hand or a flag back and forth. Wave (noun) can be a sudden surge of distress or emotion, or a fluctuation on water surface.

26   A   isle

An isle is a small island. An aisle, which is pronounced identically, is the central region between two sides of seating or two sides of items on sale.

27   E   ado

The term ado is most often used in the phrase "Without further ado," during the process of introducing a performer or speaker. Ado means fuss. Adieu, is a term for farewell arising from French.

28   A   criterion

A criterion is a requirement or standard that must be met. An individual may have to meet several criteria. Criteria can be used to categorise, but it is criteria rather than categories that are "met".

29   B   remorse

Remorse means feeling guilty or deeply regretful, for harm caused or a crime committed.

30   A   delirious

Delirious means in a state of confusion. Delirious people may have hallucinations which are false sensations (such as a the appearance of a dead person as a ghost) or say meaningless things.

1 E simplistic

Superficial means not detailed or deep, but rather casual or cursory, addressing only the simplest and outermost aspects.

2 A convenient

Expedient means convenient to achieve an aim, but with the implication that this may not be lawful, correct or ethically correct.

3 A exaggerate

Embellish is to increase attractiveness by adding details or decorations. It has a special meaning, where those decorations are untrue details added to a story, to make it more interesting.

4 C half-hearted

Grudging means reluctant, resentful and unenthusiastic. Synonyms include half-hearted, hesitant, and disinclined.

5 C cheap

Economical means costing relatively little. It does not refer to the economy as a whole, but rather to the cost to an individual or company that is paying for something.

6 A impertinent

Flippant means inappropriately light-hearted; not showing a respectful, serious attitude to a matter that is serious or important.

7 B annoying

Exasperating means very annoying or frustrating. Synonyms are maddening, enraging, infuriating, irksome.

8 D submissive

Dominant means leading or influencing others, exerting control.

9 A commonplace

Esoteric means so difficult or complex that only very few people will be able to understand. It is used to describe very specialised fields or knowledge.

10 B superstitious

Capricious means tending to have sudden changes of choice, mood or behaviour, in an unpredictable and perhaps inexplicable manner.

11 B holiday

A holiday is a trip or time off school or work (or vacation), whereas the others mean empty.

12 D lock

All the words mean bringing together, coalescence or amalgamation, except lock.

13 A triumphant

Triumphant means winning or being very happy after achieving something, whereas the other words describe courageous and good behaviour.

14 A trickling

Trickling indicates flowing very slowly or at a slow rate of fluid volume per second. The other words mean quiet and free of disturbance.

15 B fashionable
All the words mean tired or exhausted except fashionable.

16 E grassland
All the words mean disorganisation or dispute, except grassland.

17 C unwell
All the words mean weak or lacking in flavour (for example, in relation to a soup), except unwell.

18 'UERR': the word is 'guerrilla'
A guerrilla is a member of a small group fighting against a large power, implying the combat episodes are small skirmishes. The word now means any activity occurring irregularly or without warning.

19 E spoon
The implement most useful for eating chips is a fork. The instrument most useful for eating (or drinking) soup is a spoon. A ladle is usually used in preparation rather than at the dining table.

20 E pine
A leaf is one of the numerous green extremities of an oak (tree). Similarly the green extremities of a pine are called needles because of their long thin shape.

21 A invincible
If something is a duplicate, it definitely cannot be unique. If something is vulnerable (capable of being conquered or wounded) it cannot be invulnerable (incapable of being conquered or harmed).

22 D civil
Civil means polite or well-mannered. The word also is used to indicate matters that are not military. It can also indicate legal matters that are not a crime (criminal) but a dispute between two people.

23 C magnetic
Magnetic means attractive. Some metallic objects by magnetism attract other metals, or attract or repel other magnets. More generally it means able to influence others through one's personality or speech.

24 E jibe
To jibe is to agree, applied to facts rather than people. A gibe is a cheeky or mischievous remark, especially interrupting the speech of another.

25 E eludes
Elude means escape from something that is chasing. Commonly it describes a question, comment or answer that was in one's mind before but for now cannot be recalled.

26 C bolster
To bolster is to support. It is also a noun for a pillow or other similar support.

27 D licence
Licence is formal permission to do a business or another activity. Figuratively it means the freedom (of an artist, writer or poet) to depict in a manner that does not exactly reflect reality.

28 B farcical
Farcical means ridiculous or resembling a farce (a form of comedy). It is also applied to everyday activities showing poor organisation or made pointless because an important aspect has failed.

29 E serenity
Serenity means calmness and composure; tranquility and poise.

30 D disillusion
Disillusion is the disappointment when expectations have been built up to an illusory (exaggerated) level and then return to reality. Dissolution is the separation of a group into its members.

1   E   utilise

Exploit means use. It can additionally indicate that the use is unfair on the person, organisation or thing being used, e.g. Do not exploit these children's innocence by overpricing this food."

2   D   degenerate

Decadent means declining in level of culture or moral qualities. It can be applied to societies that are failing because current generations are not meeting the high standards of their predecessors.

3   D   tycoon

A magnate is a businessperson that is very powerful, influential and wealthy. Synonyms are mogul, industrialist, financier, entrepreneur.

4   B   insensitive

Crass means insensitive, (carelessly) rude, or blundering. It also implies the person is unintelligent.

5   E   effervescence

Exuberance is being very energetic, joyful and enthusiastic.

6   E   overwhelming

Insurmountable is an adjective that can be applied to a challenge that is too great to be overcome.

7   C   prevaricate

To equivocate is to make unclear or ambiguous statements, usually to avoid answering a question properly or to give a false impression and yet later be able to deny having done so intentionally.

8   A   awful

Exemplary means having the ideal features for a good example. Typically it means the item or behaviour in question is extremely good.

9   D   glorify

To denounce to publically and boldly announce that someone has done something wrong or worthless or a fake.

10   D   finish

Endeavour (verb) means try very hard to do something or achieve a goal. As a noun it means that process of trying.

11   A   mentalist

A sycophant is a person who grovels to someone important in order to advance themselves. Other synonyms are puppet, hanger-on, crawler, and leech.

12   C   oblique

Oblique means diagonal, i.e. not straight in one of the main axes such as up, down, left, right or forward or backward.

13   D   mouth

All the words mean a way of speaking, except mouth.

14   C   violent

All the words mean withdrawn, quiet and modest, except violent.

15   B   understanding
The other words all mean the build up of fear that can occur before an event.

16   A   impenetrable
All the other words mean very slight. Impenetrable means cannot be penetrated. This can be because it is very complicated (an impenetrable book) or well defended (an impenetrable castle wall).

17   E   identical
Identical means exactly the same; the other words indicate that something is not the best (and in the case of some of the words, not the worst).

18   'ALV': the word is 'halve'
Halve means to divide into two pieces. It is implied that the two pieces are equal, so that each is half of the whole.

19   C   letter
A carton is a common container for conveying juice once it has been produced (squeezed from the fruit). An envelope is a common container for conveying a letter, once it has been produced (written).

20   D   rain
A mackintosh (with a K) is a hardy, full-length, waterproof coat. Commonly the waterproofing is achieved using a layer of rubber.

21   C   ingest
If one is puzzled, one can resolve this by investigating. If one is starving, one can resolve this by ingesting (eating). One can eat a waffle, but investigate, which sets the pattern, is a verb.

22   C   liberal
Liberal means open, in policy, entrance criteria, coverage, or thought.

23   E   current
Current means flow of electricity or water or, more rarely, any other fluid. As an adjective, it means relating to the present (in contrast to the past or future).

24   A   frieze
A frieze is a long piece of decorative art on, or as part of, a wall. To freeze is to make or become very cold, so that liquid turns to solid. This term is most commonly used for water turning to ice.

25   A   dessert
Dessert is a light dish, often sweet, after a main meal. Desert (noun or adjective) is waterless land. Desert (verb) means abandon. It can be used to describe a skill or ability that vanishes when needed.

26   C   cynic
A cynic is a person who argues that most people are motivated by self-interest rather than by the desire for the common good or to spread the truth.

27   E   delineate
Delineate is to lay out in detail, or mark very clearly the outline of something (such as an area of land).

28   B   stagnant
Stagnant water lacks a current that brings in fresh water continuously, and so becomes unpleasant. Of an economy or an establishment, stagnant means not developing or being refreshed.

29   E   chortle
Chortle means laugh, or sing with intense joy.

30   D   exemplify
Exemplify means be a good example of something, epitomize or symbolise. More rarely, it can mean that a person is turning something into an example.

1   D   tribal

Ethnic means relating to a group (particularly a subgroup of a larger population) with shared culture, tradition or habits.

2   E   mean

To denote means to represent, signify or mean. It is in contrast to connote, which means to represent in a more subtle way, or to suggest without being explicit.

3   D   regard

To esteem is to hold someone in high regard, with respect or admiration. As a verb, it can mean respect or admire.

4   D   beautiful

Enchanting means very attractive, or highly favourable in behaviour.

5   B   selfish

Egotistical means concerned only with one's own well-being; selfish.

6   E   revolting

Nauseating means tending to make people vomit. It generally indicates something horrible or revolting.

7   A   untidy

Dishevelled means out of neat order. It is commonly applied to hair or clothes. A homeless person might be dishevelled but they are not synonymous.

8   B   decisive

Ambivalent means undecided between two options. It is distinct from ambiguous, which indicates a failure to describe something clearly.

9   C   rudeness

Decorum is polite and appropriate behaviour. It does not mean well decorated, organised or tidy.

10   A   contagious

Reflective means thoughtful or contemplative (in relation to people) or able to reflect light (in relation to objects).

11   A   salacious

Rapacious means very greedy. All are synonyms except for salacious (derived from "salty") which is used to refer to stories or gossip that many consider interesting because of their sexual content.

12   A   decade

A decade is ten years. All the other words mean an object or relationship that is weak, and not made of solid substance.

13   D   pester

Pester is not an adjective, while the others can be. When there appears to be no odd one out based on general meaning, look for parts of speech (noun/adjective/verb) or tenses that do not match.

14   A   illegal

Illegal means against the law, whereas the other words describe something that creates fear in the mind.

15 B atlantic

The Atlantic is an ocean. The Pacific is also an ocean, but here the word is pacific (without a capital P) which means tending to be peaceful and calm.

16 D ultimatum

An ultimatum is a requirement or demand one person places in front of another, typically with a deadline: do this by that time, or else.

17 A misplace

All the words mean move something to a different place, except misplace which means to lose something. Misplace implies accidental loss, and the object doesn't have to be moved to be misplaced.

18 'NDSO': the word is 'handsome'

Handsome means attractive in appearance, and is generally applied to males. A hansom cab was a low carriage for two passengers, with one horse, and a driver seated behind and above the carriage.

19 A water

A spark is a form in which one might see a small amount of electricity flowing. Likewise a drip is a form in which one might see a small amount of water flowing.

20 D storey

A textbook is made largely of many pages. Likewise a skyscraper is made of many storeys (with an EY), which is another word for floors or levels.

21 A silent

If something is rotating, it cannot be stationary. If something is booming (loud), it cannot be silent.

22 A alter

To alter is to modify. An altar is a table used in religious ceremonies. Although Akiko could have discarded or replaced her clothes, only "alter" fits with the sense of being to wear the same clothes.

23 D caution

Caution is the noun for being careful to avoid danger or error.

24 B freeze

To freeze is to make or become very cold, so that liquid turns to solid, especially water turning to ice. Figuratively it refers to stopping movement. A frieze is a long piece of decorative art on a wall.

25 C aberrant

Aberrant means incorrect or outside normal standards, while abhorrent indicates a strong emotional reaction such as disgust, for example in relation to a crime or harm to a creature or person.

26 A grisly

Grisly means horrible, ghastly or revolting, in relation to a crime or a scene. Gristly means containing much gristle, the stringy tissue in meat. A grizzly is a North American brown bear.

27 D brooding

Brooding means growing and nurturing someone, a young animal or (figuratively) a feeling- especially a negative one.

28 E climactic

Climactic means relating to the climax of something. Typically it relates to a moment or instant, during a sporting event, play or film, or a tense negotiation.

29 E poignancy

Poignancy means causing intense sadness. It is used to refer to a moment in time, a scene, an event or a memory. Idolatry is worship of a statue or other image of a god.

30 C enthralling

Enthralling means so interesting as to hold one's attention totally.

1   A   inflexible

Dogmatic means believing facts as being completely and obviously true; a tendency to behave as though others should also accept this.

2   E   environment

Habitat means the natural environment of a plant or animal. It is the Latin word for "it dwells", and is related to the English word "habitable", meaning possible to dwell in.

3   A   cunning

Guile means intelligence, and specifically the type that is cunning, sly or devious, rather than general intelligence or high scoring in school tests, for example.

4   E   leader

The doyen is the most expert, eminent and respected person in a particular specialty.

5   D   attenuation

Diminution means reduction in size or quantity.

6   E   meticulous

Painstaking is an adjective (not a verb) indicating that something was done with an extraordinary level of attention to detail. It does not mean actually painful.

7   D   subdue

Repress means forcefully restrain or subdue a person or population, e.g. an authoritarian government using its power to prevent opposition. In psychology it means blocking out a thought or emotion.

8   D   hasten

To dawdle is to move in a very slow, unhurried, and easily distracted way, or to pause.

9   A   admire

To deplore is to condemn something as terrible or shocking.

10   E   valiant

All the words mean arrogant or excessively proud, except valiant which means brave.

11   E   drunken

A drunken party may be raucous but raucous does not mean drunken, it means noisy, rough and discordant.

12   C   obviously

Obviously means clearly; all the other words mean unclearly or indirectly.

13   E   ship

All the words mean inflexible, harsh or severe, except ship.

14   B   sinful

All the words mean a path that is not straight but full of bends, except sinful which means committing sins or deeds considered wrong within a religion.

15   D   proud

In the usage that allows it to match the other words, vein means a strand or thread of something (such as coal or gold). The word sounding similar, meaning proud, is vain.

16   D   prosecute

Persecute means to harass and harm a person or a group of people, over a long period of time, e.g. governments mistreating large groups of people. Prosecute is to take someone to court for a crime.

17   C   drilling

Drilling is a method of making a hole, as is boring, but boring is also synonymous with all the other words that mean uninteresting.

18   'ELET': the word is 'omelette'

This idiom means that to achieve an important end, it might be necessary to do something damaging at the beginning.

19   E   old

If something is concise it has achieved brevity. If someone is old he or she has achieved longevity.

20   C   dawn

Dusk is the intermediate period between full daylight ending and full nighttime taking hold. Dawn, similarly, is the period between night and the next day.

21   C   ignore

If the lighting in a room is darkened, it is does the opposite of dazzle. To harken is to take note of; the opposite is to ignore.

22   E   adopt

Adopt is to receive something and treat it as one's own: e.g. a child or a habit. Adapt is to change something. If both fit, think whether the thing being received is being changed before being used?

23   A   distinct

Distinct means different as an entity or different in nature from other similar entities. It also means having a clear boundary. Separately it also means readily sensed, such as a distinct smell.

24   C   allusion

Allusion means a reference to something that is indirect, subtle or unclear. Illusion means deceptive appearance. Elision is omission of some words or characters, for example "don't" from "do not."

25   D   cereal

Cereal is a type of breakfast. Serial means one after another; as a noun it can be applied to anything (such a book, film or story) that emerges in this way.

26   E   borne

Borne is the past tense of bear. The parents or school have to bear the costs, so the costs must be borne.

27   E   navel

Watch out for the E versus the A. The navel is the umbilicus or belly button. Naval means in relation to ships or a navy.

28   B   demure

Demure means shy and not outgoing. Diminutive means small. A small person might be demure but does not have to be. To demur is to disagree.

29   E   charlatan

A charlatan is person who pretends to have a skill or knowledge; a con artist.

30   A   dissolution

Dissolution is the breaking up of a group into individual members. It is different from disillusion which is the sense of disappointment when it is realised that high expectations will not be met.

1   B   describe

Most commonly recount means simply tell the story (an account) of what happened. Sometimes it means literally re-count, i.e. repeat a count, for example after a closely contested election.

2   D   intermittent

Episodic means in a series of episodes, interrupted by gaps when it is not taking place. It is the opposite of continuous.

3   D   dedicated

Earnest means intense, dedicated and hardworking.

4   D   era

Epoch means a (very long) period of time. The word is also sometimes used to indicate a short period of time, but only when a clear statement is made to indicate this.

5   A   complaint

Gripe means minor complaint, or to complain repeatedly, especially about a minor problem.

6   B   redundant

Superfluous means unnecessary in the sense of being extra to what is already present which is already sufficient.

7   E   unsettled

Perturbed means upset or disturbed by an event, person or thing. It has the implication that the disturbance has interfered with one's activities.

8   C   glee

Disdain is contempt for something or someone: a sensation that they are beneath one in quality.

9   B   convene

To disband is to split up a group into its constituent parts. This is particularly used of a group of people who stop being a group and go their own ways.

10   D   announce

Retract and the other words mean to take something back or undo it; to announce does not have that meaning.

11   A   uplift

Uplift means cheer up, whereas revive means bring back to life (from sleep or near death).

12   A   piggish

All the words indicate someone who cheats, except piggish which means like a pig.

13   A   miser

A miser is someone who does not want to spend money, despite having a great deal of money.

14   A   ravenous

Other than ravenous, which means extremely hungry, the other words mean having an illness.

15   E   honest

Moral versus morale. Moral (adjective) means regarding the distinction between good and bad behaviour. Moral (noun) is the lesson from a story or experience. Morale is confidence or enthusiasm within a group.

16   C   spittle

All the words mean unkind and vicious, except spittle which mean saliva.

17   E   lava

Lava is the molten rock that flows from an actual volcano. All the other terms are used to describe someone who occasionally becomes extremely angry.

18   'UORE': the word is 'fluorescent'

Fluorescent means giving off its own light, after being stimulated by electricity or by another form or colour of light or other type of energy.

19   B   murder

A butt of a joke is the person injured by the joke. A victim is the person injured by the murder. Only if the question had stated joker (a person) might the answer be criminal (a person).

20   E   cheek

A bulge is seen on the surface of the body in relation to the activity of a muscle. A dimple is a depression seen on the surface of the body when the cheek is active, such as in smiling.

21   E   aspiring

An arrow or other sign is often pointing in a direction. Likewise, if one has an ambition, one is aspiring to it (i.e. aiming or desiring to achieve it).

22   D   effected

Effected means achieved or performed. Affected means changed or influenced or (more rarely) faked or generated artificially.

23   D   days'

Even adults find this difficult. Give notice of 3 days. If something is of 3 days, it is like something of 3 boys. It is written 3 days', just as it would be written 3 boys'.

24   E   gibe

A gibe is a cheeky or mischievous remark, especially interrupting the speech of another. To jibe is to agree, applied to facts rather than people.

25   C   burglar

A burglar is a person who enters a building without permission and steals from it. The term is distinct from robber, where there is an attack on a person rather than on a building.

26   C   borne

Confusingly, both "born" and "borne" can relate to childbirth. "Born" is what has happened to the baby. "Borne" is what the mother has done during the pregnancy, the process of bearing the child.

27   D   deference

Deference is the outward manifestation of respect and submission for another person, typically more senior or high-ranking within an organisation or family.

28   B   broach

To broach is to open discussion of a subject, or to break down a wall or barrier. Unrelated, a brooch, pronounced identically, is a piece of jewellery, typically worn on the front of a blouse or coat.

29   B   gristly

Gristly means containing much gristle, the less edible stringy or elastic connective tissue in a piece of meat. Grizzly is a North American brown bear. Grisly means horrible, ghastly or revolting.

30   E   invigilate

To invigilate is to supervise the sitting of an exam, ensuring that the pupils have appropriate conduct and do not cheat.

The Non-Verbal Ninja

Intensive Training through *Visual* Explanations

Comprehensive course from basics to advanced puzzles

Answers and explanations given graphically

3-volume set systematically tackling the numerous CEM puzzle types

600 questions designed to build efficient strategies for success

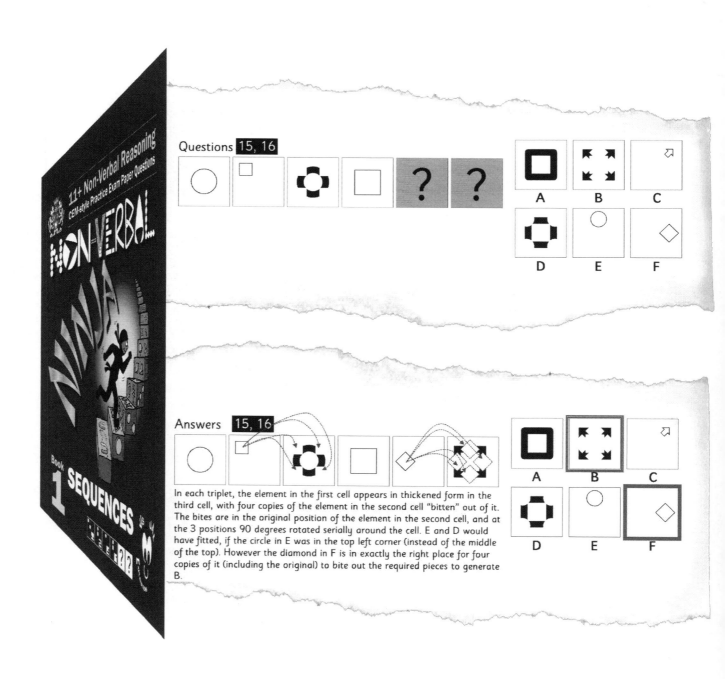

11+ Non-Verbal Reasoning
CEM-style Practice Exam Paper Questions

NON-VERBAL NINJA

Book 1 SEQUENCES

Questions 15, 16

Answers 15, 16

In each triplet, the element in the first cell appears in thickened form in the third cell, with four copies of the element in the second cell "bitten" out of it. The bites are in the original position of the element in the second cell, and at the 3 positions 90 degrees rotated serially around the cell. E and D would have fitted, if the circle in E was in the top left corner (instead of the middle of the top). However the diamond in F is in exactly the right place for four copies of it (including the original) to bite out the required pieces to generate B.

Questions 29, 30

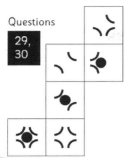

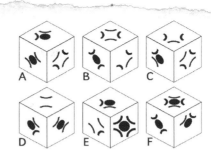

A B C

D E F

Answers 29, 30

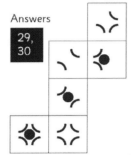

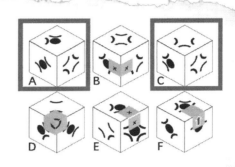

A B C

D E F

Question 13

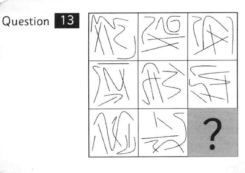

?

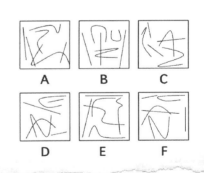

A B C

D E F

Answer 13

Each cell has three straight lines and three curved lines. In the top row, all crossings are between two straight lines. In the bottom row, all crossings are between two curved lines.

In the middle row, all crossings are between a curved and a straight line. In the left column, there is 1 crossing. In the middle, there are 2. In the right column, there are 3.

 Too many crossings
 Wrong type of crossings
 Wrong type of crossings

D
 Too many of the lines are curved
 Too few crossings

Printed in Great Britain
by Amazon